YOU ARE YOUR OWN

Million Dollar Formula

YOU ARE AMAZING. REMEMBER, YOU HAVE EVERYTHING
YOU NEED TO **ACHIEVE ANYTHING YOU WANT!**

Nic Cunningham and Ali Villani
the Entrepreneurial Babes

BALBOA.
PRESS
A DIVISION OF HAY HOUSE

Balboa Press books may be ordered through booksellers or by contacting:

Balboa Press
A Division of Hay House
1663 Liberty Drive
Bloomington, IN 47403
www.balboapress.com.au
1 (877) 407-4847

Because of the dynamic nature of the Internet, any web addresses or links contained in this book may have changed since publication and may no longer be valid. The views expressed in this work are solely those of the author and do not necessarily reflect the views of the publisher, and the publisher hereby disclaims any responsibility for them.

The author of this book does not dispense medical advice or prescribe the use of any technique as a form of treatment for physical, emotional, or medical problems without the advice of a physician, either directly or indirectly. The intent of the author is only to offer information of a general nature to help you in your quest for emotional and spiritual well-being. In the event you use any of the information in this book for yourself, which is your constitutional right, the author and the publisher assume no responsibility for your actions.

Any people depicted in stock imagery provided by Thinkstock are models, and such images are being used for illustrative purposes only.
Certain stock imagery © Thinkstock.

Print information available on the last page.

ISBN: 978-1-5043-0221-0 (sc)
ISBN: 978-1-5043-0222-7 (e)

Balboa Press rev. date: 10/25/2016

CONTENTS

PREFACE

This book is for you, for your career, for your divine purpose, and for all the opportunities you are trying to create for yourself but have not been able to manifest. We have created this book with the intention of providing a template and road map for individual success and financial independence for empowered women. Together and independently, we have coached and mentored thousands of women with innovative ideas, inspiration, creativity, passion and drive, who were unable to create financial freedom for themselves. These women were talented and connected beyond all reason, but they were blocked personally and spiritually, unable to make that transition to financial freedom.

We believe there has been no greater time in history when our planet needs women to step up into their divine expressions and be the truest and purest expressions, living in authenticity. Women are leaders and visionaries who come from the heart space. Through the empowerment and leadership of women, our world can and will change; it's now time to claim the space around this. Healing and abundance will pour out over each continent, run through the rivers and streams, and head out to the ocean like never before. We are the change that Mother Nature has been calling for—an academy of spiritually attuned and divinely purposed empowered women, on a mission to express their gifts and grace in order to create global impact and change.

Financial independence creates the opportunity for women to splash their creativity and purpose into the world without any limitations. They have the opportunity to create a difference, to teach, to lead, and to create legacies that will continue beyond them. As we coach and mentor you in the coming chapters, we will break down the limitations and barriers that you have created for yourself. We will assist you to step up into the entrepreneurial dream you have in your heart. We will teach you how to build wealth, sink deep into your truth, inspire others, and create personal and financial freedom and the lifestyle you want for you, and the people you care about.

Are you ready to step up, claim the space, and be the best version of yourself? You are your own million dollar formula, so let's see your life change before your eyes! We are so excited to share this journey with you.

PART ONE

Create

The first step towards getting somewhere is to decide that you are not going to stay where you are.

—J.P Morgan

CHAPTER 1

Deciding to Love Yourself

*W*hat do you believe you are here for? Let yourself think and dream really big for a moment. What do you believe you are destined for? If you had a magic wand, there were no limitations, and you could wave that wand to achieve and create anything that was in your heart, what would you create? What ideas, innovations, creativity, and talents have been placed in your path? In your heart, what project keeps giving you the universal nudge?

Most of your limitations and self-put-downs are a result of you not dreaming or thinking big enough. At some point in your life, perhaps in your childhood or on your journey, a story with limitations was planted in your mind. Maybe it's a belief about your potential. Maybe you were told you weren't good enough. Maybe it was a comment from a parent, teacher, or someone else of influence.

Up to this point, if you have not acted on your ideas or your innovations, we can put money on the fact that you are living "in the story." What we mean by this is that you are living out the circumstances and limitations of the judgements or comments that have been previously made about you.

What if we challenged you to say that you are bigger than this story? You have an unlimited resource of talent, ideas, knowledge, creativity, and ability to manifest every one of your business goals and projects. We will help stretch you to be the leader and entrepreneur you desire to be.

These limitations and negative beliefs that go on in your mind are a program that has been playing over and over and over in your life and in every element of your consciousness. It can work for you, and it can most definitely work against you. Just like everything in our lives, we can create positivity and opportunity, or we can create stagnation and suffering for ourselves.

Most of us are completely unaware of the programming dictating our behaviours, our relationships, and the opportunities that show up in our lives. The greatest way to understand and identify what programs are on rerun in your life is to see what you're surrounded by. For example, are you surrounded by lack? Do you never have enough time, enough money, enough resources, enough of anything? This indicates there is a program playing called "never having enough." Is your life representative of emotional pain and betrayal in your relationships, or do you experience great pain and conflict in your relationships? If this is the program that is playing out for you, it suggests that the program on rerun is "I'm always alone" or "relationships are difficult."

Identifying the recurrent themes of suffering in your life helps you piece together the program. Once this is pieced together, you can spend some time working out where it came from. Knowing this is interesting to identify, but it is not essential for you to remove the program from your life and recoup behaviours it triggers in you.

Nic had a program that caused her great anguish, drama, and financial loss for a very long time. The limiting belief and program that she played in her life was one of not being lovable. This played out in her life by having many broken relationships, including a divorce—and only a few years later, she had another painful separation. It wasn't until this program became really painful, and Nic was tipped to breaking point, that she identified the patterns and programming that were playing out. It's often the case that we have to hit an emotional pain point before we're willing to see what has been in front of us all the time.

Identifying the program and where it came from enabled Nic to regroup and reprogram her beliefs about herself. She consciously made efforts, grew into a loving relationship with herself, and healed and reprogrammed her life. She was then able to express that she is and always has been lovable. The result of this reprogramming and growth is that she now enjoys a beautiful relationship of love with herself.

Similarly, Ali was living out the story of ill health. Ali had lived with poor health for most of her adult life: undiagnosed coeliac disease; a long, hard road of infertility; a complete hysterectomy at thirty-six years old; and a neurological disorder were part of her experience. Ali was doing all she knew. She always had an internal lean towards the natural therapies but had never met anyone who could fill in the gaps, produce the results, or provide the education that could help her make different choices.

Most people can't begin to think of the medical expenses associated with the story Ali was playing out, let alone the mental and emotional costs over those years. You can't do better until you know better. It was through meeting Nic and having an intense session that things began to change for Ali.

Ali now enjoys incredible and radiant health. Also, the health of her children has transformed as a result of Nic's coaching and the shift in mindset associated with the story she had always told herself. As Ali studied the mind-body connection and undertook years of challenging personal development, her limiting beliefs shifted, and the story she once played out no longer fit. Ali believes in her body's ability to heal itself. She believes and knows intimately the personal power and freedom that comes from living in and stepping up to her creativity.

We laugh as we share the story of our first coaching session together. Nic hit Ali with a pen and wouldn't stop. She kept tapping on her knee with a metal pen, asking Ali, "How long are you going to let me do this? This is no different from the story you are living out about your health. Clearly it hurts; clearly there is suffering as you sit in front of me with jerks, twitches, numbness, and fatigue. You can choose to continue living this story and experiencing the same suffering, or you can leave this building right now, choosing something different." Nic worked with Ali for a little under twelve months, and all of Ali's symptoms resolved. Ali's commitment to making better choices about her health is serving her greatly. Ali is now able to keep up with Nic's intensity, including the international travel schedule that we have. She is on fire. She looks and feels great.

> *I am becoming the healthiest person I can be. A healthy body is the foundation of my success.*

At any time we can decide to detach and grow into a new program. However, we would really love for you to choose this now. Why? Because it will cost you far less time and suffering if you begin this process sooner rather than later. In all honesty, your greatest dreams and your infinite wealth and business success lie on the other side of this reprogramming. This may sound complicated and difficult, but it is simply about awareness and choice.

So let's get back to the basics. You are here to enjoy huge success, to have an affluent lifestyle, and to be loved and rewarded for all you do. You are here to make a big difference to the world. How many of you believe us when we say this? If your answer is no, there is a program that needs to be altered.

What if you just pretend to believe us, and allow yourself to truly dream with that magic wand about what your life can be once you reprogram it? Of all the programs that run in the background, like the CD that keeps skipping at the same point each time, is self-love.

After coaching thousands of women around the world, we see the biggest program with limitations concerns self-love. Maybe you've been told that to love yourself means you are stuck up or conceited. Maybe you were accused of big-noting yourself when you celebrated an achievement. All of these can influence the beliefs and ideas you have about yourself. We hate to break it to you, but it's all a farce. It is nonsense that we have been fed generation after generation. It's like the myth that we shouldn't eat eggs because they contain too much cholesterol.

You are perfect, talented, lovable, and designed to be the greatest success your life has ever seen. The sooner you change your program to this one instead of the old, annoying CD that plays, "I'm not good enough. I'm not pretty enough. I'm not unique or clever enough," the sooner your life will change. The day you understand this and consciously choose to be 100 per cent your authentic self and the best version of you that you can be, acting on all your divine gifts and creativity—that will be the day your business, your innovative idea, or your product begins to make money! Not only will you experience financial freedom, but you'll step into a personal freedom like never before. Why is this the case? You and your business are your self-worth. If you don't believe that you can, or if you don't believe it is possible because of a limiting program, what product or business you are trying to launch is completely irrelevant.

Your success in business is directly linked to your personal success, which is birthed in self-worth and self-belief. This is why it's so important for you to kick those old programs to the kerb and abandon and disconnect from the judgements, criticisms, and projected thoughts of others. Choose to love yourself. Yes, we said it: you must choose to love yourself and be yourself.

The reason we say you must choose this is because there are plenty of opportunities out there in the world that would like you to choose otherwise. Look at the thousands of advertisements in women's magazines trying to sell you concealer, or the weight-loss advertisements telling you that your success is related to your cup size. What a load of rubbish! You have been perfect from your first breath. Your parents thought so, and your doting aunties and uncles and your big sister thought so too. Every milestone that you made—walking, talking, running in the school athletics carnival—made you even more amazing every day. Then you finished high school, landed your first job, and finished university, which made you even more incredible. Next, you may have become a mum, and you really stepped into a new level of awesomeness. Now you are trying to launch and scale your business or your career, and every day you become more and more amazing!

Do you feel that? Do you feel that love come up from the heart space as you realise that you truly are perfection? Now, let us challenge you to really step into this perfection and decide right now that you are awesome, you are enough, and you have never been more on fire or more prepared to take your life and business to the next level.

After we have established that you are enough, and you continue to unravel any remaining programs along the way, what is it that you are trying to do? What impact are you trying to create, what legacy are you trying to leave, and what solution are you providing to one of the world's problems? I bet you haven't stopped to ask yourself this. We know we sure hadn't! If we were really honest with ourselves, the reason was because we had not allowed ourselves to dream, and maybe we were even a little too scared to dream.

> *As I commit to loving myself, I learn I have all that*
> *I need to fulfil my dreams.*

Picture yourself storeys above where you are right now, with your business, your family, and your community. Go higher and higher until you can see the country you live in, and then go even higher, where you can sit out in a rocket ship looking back on the earth. See the beautiful blues and greens of the water and the land. Now that you are away from limitations, truly ask yourself, "What am I trying to do? What is my business about? What is the identity and concept that I am trying to create? What is my divine purpose?"

Before you brush this off and shut down, we challenge you to think and be bigger than what you have previously been able to achieve for yourself. You see, we have to stretch and get clarity before we come back and start engaging in the "doing" of being in business.

Divine purpose is the same as your identity. What makes your heart sing? What makes you happy and feel fulfilled? You know—the kind of fulfilment that if the world stopped spinning tomorrow and it was all over, you would be content. This is the activity that when you do it, nothing else matters.

Many of us who are mothers will say, "It's my children. That is what it's about." Yes, we all love our kids, but seriously, what is deeper? What is that burning desire that sits deep within you that you have to create? What is 100 per cent your own project, and what is going to be your contribution to the world?

We are all creators. We are here to create in our own unique individuality and to live a life of service, expressing that creativity. Your business is an extension of this creativity and is the birthplace of your divine purpose. When these are aligned, success and opportunities are effortless. Your business and what you are creating is your divine purpose, your divine expression of yourself. Surely this is something worth spending some time dreaming on and getting clarity about, so where did you place that magic wand?

Once you have connected with this and decided to love yourself, it's time to get clarity and decide what you want. What is it that you want, and will you be happy if you have achieved it? This is a loaded question, we know. However, without knowing what you really want, you can't put together a plan to achieve it or receive the necessary help along the way.

> *All your dreams can come true if you have the courage to pursue them.*
>
> *—Walt Disney*

Many of us think we know what we want, but we are stuck in our limitations and what we think we deserve. When you're without limitations, having chosen to love and be yourself and to let go of those programs, what do you really want? With no limitations, allow yourself to explore what happiness and success really does look like for you. This means stretching yourself and your goals to your level of discomfort. We do this every single month in our businesses as we continue to stretch ourselves to our discomfort, where our self-belief is challenged.

What does your life and business look like with no limitations? What are you doing every day? Are you working in your business, are you working on your business, or do you have a residual setup that enables you to sit on a beach in the Bahamas managing it from your laptop? What is your ultimate lifestyle and business creation? This is where the clarity comes.

Let's face it: not many of us step up into business and self-employment to work hard and have no life. However, we coach women who are slaves to their businesses and feed the dinosaurs they have created; they are not in much of a better lifestyle or financial situation than when they were working for someone else, doing a job they loved. What goes wrong in scenarios like this is there is no time placed into the big vision at the beginning of the business development. This charts a course which is set and pursued before the clarity is made. Ask yourself, "What is the outcome that I am seeking from working in and on my own business? What is the story of entrepreneurship I am creating, and what does the outcome and results look like after all of my exertion and creativity?"

If you are at the point where you are contemplating business, it's safe to say that you have made the decision for yourself that life is not just about mortgage payments, a nine to five job, and then dying. What are you really, truly trying to create? For some this is lifestyle, for others it may be job security, and for some it may be about making a global impact. Where is your heart leading you with your business? Write down what is coming up for you as we share this. This is the clarity that is needed before a business plan, or the Entrepreneurial Babes Success Template, can be put into place. Once this clarity is created, we can then encourage and coach you to be an entrepreneur, not just a dinosaur feeder! Entrepreneurship is most importantly about stepping into the visionary, leader, and industry specialist that is within you, where there are no dinosaurs!

You may doubt your ability to get this clarity, but we all have it when we connect with what feels good. It really is as simple as sticking to what feels good! What feels good is right, and what brings happiness brings self-love, which brings success.

How many times have you been close to that point of brilliance where you are happy in flow and in creation, and it feels good— but then you sabotage it by overthinking and making it harder for yourself? Many women we work with see their businesses as only an intellectual pursuit, and they get stuck in the mental game of thinking that it has to be hard or complex. Instead, we challenge them to do what feels good. When things feel good, we open up a range of experiences that can be effortless and come with ease.

Life and business have growth as part of the plan, however it doesn't have to be hard, it doesn't have to be complicated, and it should feel good. When you think about your business, your product, or your innovative idea, does it feel good? Does it make you happy and resonate to the higher purpose we have spoken about? If so, then that is where it is—that is the sweet spot. That happiness and good feeling is where we encourage you to stay, because it encourages you to be intuitive and discerning. In some ways, this good feeling can be an internal barometer. We say to our clients, "If it doesn't feel right, then change it." Women are so intuitive and heart centred. If this good feeling cannot be maintained all of the time as a guide for the best decision-making, then we really are not leaning on our greatest asset. This is not to say we don't listen to our heads, create intellectual decisions, and think things through. We are merely stating that women have an incredible ability to feel their way into their business successes, and it can be done by getting to know this good feeling.

Some people talk about a gut feeling, a knowingness, or a deep intelligence. This may be the same for most, but not for all. The feeling of good versus bad is much more obvious and is easier for us to track as a tool and barometer for our steps towards success.

When you get this good feeling, stick to it!

As I commit to being the best version of myself, success flows effortlessly from all directions.

We are all creative and have a creative contribution to make to the planet. Nic found this hard to understand for herself. She felt that she had been forgotten when the creative talents in relation to business were handed out. However, stepping into the coaching and mentoring role for so many women over the years has proven Nic wrong. What she has learned is that all businesses are expressions of creativity. She had misunderstood what creativity can be.

Nic thought that creativity meant pursuing dance, writing, music, or the arts. However, inner creativity, drive, and passion are expressions of creativity that can be expressed even in the most mathematical businesses, such as software, mechanics, and machinery. Every entrepreneur we have ever met has had two major qualities: they have been creative in their own unique way, and they have had eccentricities. We see the latter as the best qualities of all, because it makes people want to join with them, work with them, and work for them.

Nic had always been called eccentric. She remembers vividly being at college in her early twenties and being told by an older, mature student that she was the most eccentric person he had ever met. Nic took offence at this for many years; it became another one of those stories and programs that created limitations in her work, and therefore it was an obstacle to success. Similarly, Nic had never seen herself as creative. Sure, she'd played music and sung during her school years, however since graduating university and "growing up," who had time for such pursuits when trying to balance a family and a career? Boy, was she wrong! Not only is her eccentricity one of her greatest assets, but it draws people to her. People want to be around her and work for her; that was one of the major reasons that Ali wanted to partner with her. Can you see how limiting and damaging these programs can be?

Being eccentric in Nic's full expression is being a workaholic, pathologically driven, assertive, and straight down the line. How can these things be anything other than assets as an entrepreneur? You see, it's simply the label and the judgement you give it. Similarly to Ali, Nic is very creative; she has skills in marketing, communication, writing, and articulating her ideas. All of these make up her unique, aspirational design. These skills are actually being creative—they simply aren't wrapped up in the typical package we imagine creativity looks like.

Ali's creativity is far more obvious. She sings and carries every colour of highlighter with her to any meeting. She can paint, fix anything, and generally lend a hand to anything, including sewing, cooking, and drawing. When Ali was a young girl, she would carry around a box of sixty-four Derwent pencils. Ali has always had an eccentricity with her fashion and design. She has vivid memories of sewing her own patchwork flares, and of unstitching her red tabbed jeans and stitching blue velvet panels into them to make flares. Man, what a look!

We are sure that if you have been led to pick up and read this book, you also have flare and creativity that you probably have not begun to understand or explore. Your creativity may be obvious like Ali's, or it may need some thought like Nic. We are also willing to bet that this creativity is linked to your business idea, innovation, or product that you are bringing to the marketplace.

Learning about this creativity and harnessing the energy and the inspiration that it brings will be the catalyst to your fundamental message that your business conveys with the world, as well as the roll-out of your marketing. Understanding that you are creative, stepping into this expression, and validating your strengths also helps with those old limiting beliefs.

Take a few minutes and ask yourself where your creativity lies. Most of this creativity can be found in the happiness that you already have in your life. When you express this inner creativity, you feel joyful and are validated by others. This expression of creativity makes you feel free. It may be packaged as your skill set or an innate gift you have with language, with drawing, or with understanding how something works. It will most likely be in the way that you see or understand something differently than those around you. Can you see this is why it is your strength? When you begin to capitalise on these strengths, you have a million dollar formula of expression that is part of the road to your success. This is your own, unique individual expression and contribution to the planet—that divine purpose we have spoken about. Once you have identified this creativity and where you gain your enjoyment, you can capitalise on it, you can foster and nurture it, and you can stretch it and add value to it by refining its expression or skills.

Learning to outwardly channel this creativity is the key for successful entrepreneurs. Many women are trapped in the back end of their businesses, outside of their skill sets. They begin to resent their business, their staff, and their financial standing. This situation is an expression of trapped creativity; the creativity is being channelled inwardly, creating internal blocks and resistance. These blocks can be seen as anger, frustration, and resentment. Are you feeling any of these? With coaching, we can turn these businesses around. We re-engage these women with their creativity and teach them how to strengthen the support around them. This support enables them to stay in their strengths and outwardly and consistently channel their creativity. Once this is achieved, the emotions of the business transform rapidly, and so do the financials.

What we have shared so far can be summed up as follows. *You are your business*. Your creativity and flow is directly related to your profitability. Your limiting beliefs and active programs are keeping you in a story of suffering and lack, ultimately costing you happiness and money.

As you step into your creativity, align with your divine purpose and commit to listening to the universal nudges that you are receiving, then the cash will flow, the phone will ring, the sales will come, and you'll have further opportunities for success and income generation. Staying in this creative flow ensures that you are fulfilled and challenged. It also ensures that you do not get stuck feeding any dinosaurs! Financial freedom enables you to contribute to the security, legacy, and empowerment of those around you, those in your community, and globally as part of the big picture.

We are passionate about coaching women. We see the transformation in people's lives that come from challenging businesswomen to stay in their creativity. This in turn improves communities and paves the way to global improvements and sustainability of resources. However, none of this can be done without you being willing to step up and take action. We have challenged you already with a few principles, and by now you will have realised that we are straight shooters and there is minimal fluff. If you want someone to listen to your sob story, we are not of much value. We are into creating entrepreneurs and abundance and getting the job done!

Maybe you are reading this but feel lost, frustrated, and angry that the money gods have not blessed your business. Maybe you are exhausted from flogging that dead horse of a business, and it feels like a noose around your neck. We believe this is the best place to be because it's the place where you are willing to receive and be challenged about what you have been creating, and where you are committed to learning a better and more fruitful way to become your own million dollar formula.

> *Negativity may knock on your door but it doesn't mean you have to let it in.*

> *—Unknown*

We live in a time where mental illnesses—including anxiety, depression, loneliness, sadness, grief, and other low-vibrational emotions—are dominant. When you commit to exploring your creativity and engage in expressing it, your individual flow is created. We think of it as a hose. When the hose has no kinks in it and water is turned on at the tap, the outcome is a beautiful, strong stream of water that flows outside of the hose and onto the garden, nurturing all of the plants. However, if the hose has kinks in it, then Houston, we have a problem. The outcome is no flow, and the garden will stay dry or only receive a few drops.

Your creativity is your divine gift; it is your soul's signature and your vibrational blueprint that you are here to live out. Resistance and constraints around this creativity can lead to creativity being expressed inwardly rather than outwardly. When creativity is expressed inwardly, it can lead to feelings and thoughts of self-doubt, self-loathing, comparison to others, and self-criticism. We see women who are imploding emotionally; like the hose that has a big kink in it where the water cannot flow, they have a block in the flow of their creativity.

If you can resonate with those negative emotions that we just listed, we encourage you to ask yourself, "Am I imploding as a result of my creativity being channelled inwardly and not outwardly?" With awareness, now you can remove the kinks in the hose and get into watering and growing that beautiful garden, which is your divinely purposed projects, businesses, relationships, and opportunities.

When something feels good, keep doing it, stay with it, and commit to this expression of creativity. Commit to the flow of outwardly expressing your creativity. Be aware of times in your life when you may feel stuck and plagued by recurring behaviours. If you quickly remedy this, it will correct your flow.

We live in a time where we are emotionally burdened like never before. It seems that we all know people who have been categorised or labelled with a mental illness. Perhaps this is even you.

Nic has spent thirteen years specialising in the rehabilitation of mental and physical illnesses. We want to acknowledge the professionals and the role they play in supporting people with mental illness. We want to also share our perspective, which is based on thousands of cases in Nic's clinic over thirteen years.

We would never encourage someone with a mental illness to discontinue a treatment plan that has been outlined by health care professionals. Instead we hope to plant a few seeds of thought for you to mull over.

In Nic's clinic and during our coaching, we have seen women who have blocks in their creativity. It is our observation that being stuck at such a fundamental level of the self, often where the place of identity lies, can be a trigger for (if not a cause of) mental and emotional imbalance.

What we observe in the women that we help to rehabilitate is when this aspect of the self is acknowledged and nurtured, they can return to a state of joy and happiness. In our opinion, anxiety, depression, being overwhelmed, low self-worth, and internal emptiness can occur when a person's true identity is inhibited. This inhibition can be by the person themselves, it can be a projection by others, or it can be a result of a self-limiting belief or program that is running in the individual's mindset.

Ali's story is one example of this. Ali was a gifted and creative person who was also very talented academically. As a result of her academic talent, she was discouraged from pursuing her creativity. When she began to consciously repress her creativity, these feelings of low self-worth, lack of identity, and even mental illness crept in. The consequence of this trapped creativity was years of self-medicating with alcohol and emotionally shutting down. It took years of personal development, challenging these thoughts, and changing her reoccurring behaviour to break out of this program. Ali says that when she suppressed her creativity, it was like her colourful Derwent pencils had all turned black. She was trapped within herself, within her locked creativity. Once she corrected it, her life opened up, and she began to see colour again. Nic observes that when Ali continues to step up and claim the space around her creativity, being the best version of herself in her creativity, she becomes more authentic. Not only does this invite further opportunity for flow and creativity, but it also creates an infinite influx of new income.

The conscious exertion and pursuit of this inner creativity to find joy, find meaning, and express their unique blueprint is such an incredible tool of transformation. For some women, it can be as simple as giving inner permission to follow a passion. For others, we have seen this change as a commitment to paint, sing, write, dance, or connect with others.

Many metaphysical authors have written about the mind-body connection. We now have more information than ever before, as well as research understanding the roles of the nervous system and specific hormones that create the feelings of happiness and well-being. We want to encourage those who may be living in this internal struggle with blocked creativity, and those who may have even been categorised as having depression or anxiety, to spend some time reflecting about the possibility of blocked creativity.

What are the costs of blocked creativity? There are costs to our health and well-being, as well as costs to our relationships and wealth. When we are blocked and have negative feelings, emotions, and thoughts, every aspect of our lives is infected. By transforming our attitude to one of actively expressing creativity may be the beginning of changing our mindset, thoughts, and emotions.

Nic likes to use this exercise with the women in her clinic. Close your eyes, and at every moment you feel that inner stooge, that negativity, and that overwhelm, ask yourself two simple questions: "What do I need? What do I want?" Returning to this very essence of the self can occur after just a moment of practicing this mindfulness. You have the opportunity to realign and adjust your experience. You have the opportunity to make a different choice, a choice towards creativity and being the most truthful expression of yourself.

The challenge with these emotions and a mind-body imbalance is that they can occur in the background of your consciousness. We will explore this in the third part of the book, where we will explain the role and the power of the subconscious and conscious minds. However, for now, this simple exercise of centering yourself and reconnecting to your wants and needs at any given moment gives you an opportunity to pursue your creativity. Your creativity is what brings you joy, what makes a smile come across your face, and what connects you to this inner divinity and purpose for which you are here.

Nic likes to practice this mindfulness with her cup of coffee every morning. As she sits and sips her coffee, she consciously connects within and asks herself, "What do I need? What do I want?" This is a wonderful reminder and ceremony to start each day. Consciously set the intention to stay connected with the creativity that brings joy and expression, despite what happens in the day. Know that you can return to this place at any moment by closing your eyes, connecting with the breath, and asking those two questions, which can bring you back at any moment to expressing the best and most truthful version of yourself in all that comes before you, including in relationships and business.

Ali also uses the technique of asking herself two questions as a practice of mindfulness. Ali uses it as a way of keeping herself on task and in her true creativity. She uses it whenever she experiences feelings of overwhelm, finds herself distracted, and needs to refocus her energy throughout the day onto the correct task.

When we consistently choose to express our inner creativity, we remain connected to joy, happiness, and fulfilment.

When I step up and claim the success in my business,
I see the positives changes in the world around me.

Now is the time to be truly honest with yourself. Challenge yourself to take some action. Are you only doing what you love in your business? How connected are you to your creativity, and how much do you allow yourself to enjoy it? Are you a person who needs to outsource, who needs to realign your energy and your time so that you can connect within? Connecting and expressing your creativity is *not* indulgent. It is the beginning of a unique, deep, and prolonged ease in your business that will begin to materialise miracles and wealth into all aspects of your life.

What is resonating with you so far? Are you willing to be honest with yourself about where you are spending your energy? If you were to give yourself a score out of ten for the joy and happiness you have in your work life, what would it be? It's worth applying this exercise to the other aspects of your life too. What would you score yourself as a partner, as a mother, as a sister, as a daughter, and as a friend? Are you depleted and overwhelmed in any of these areas?

We specialise in transforming business and preventing entrepreneurial burnout. This exercise is critical in identifying where the leaks are. Where is your creativity being zapped? Are you continually putting out fires in your life and business, or are you building your empire gracefully? The incredible thing is that business can be effortless when you choose it to be so.

Choose to live as your unique self, expressing your divine creativity in every aspect of your life. That mindset expands the joy, happiness, and wealth you receive. You can have effortlessness everywhere. Why do you need to make your entrepreneurial pursuit hard? Why can't it be effortless, creative, and fulfilling?

> *I love myself and my business. Income and opportunity flow effortlessly to me now and always.*

We can tell you that our lives were not always like this! We used to live and work in resistance. We experienced these feelings and were thrown around by the situations in our businesses. Not anymore! We are more empowered and accountable entrepreneurs than we were ten years ago. We are in constant accountability to ourselves and to each other about our connection to creativity. We live in this expression of creativity. Anything that does not look and feel like this creativity is not in our lives. We no longer pursue anything that doesn't feel and look like the best and truest versions of ourselves.

Now, this doesn't mean that we have become space cadets. We are not wasting time or just going with the flow—to the contrary, we are completely in control of ourselves. As we have mastered this technique of staying centred in our creative expression, we are no longer firefighters in our lives. Problems can still arise, however they are far less often and much less intense than they used to be. There is an ease and a grace to our lives, to our entrepreneurial pursuits, that was not there years ago.

The biggest change is that we have chosen inner joy and happiness as the barometer for our entrepreneurial pursuits. If it doesn't make our hearts sing, then we don't do it. We have learnt to outsource to people who love doing what we don't. At what point did that program, saying we have to be good at everything, begin? The truth is that no one is perfect, and we spend a lot of energy and exertion trying to chase perfection. Just like the pot of gold at the end of the rainbow, perfection doesn't exist. What does exist is internal peace and internal fulfilment, which come from stepping into our unique creativity.

Another thought for you to contemplate is energetic and financial leakage. How much time do you spend flogging that dead horse? What part of your business doesn't come easily for you? For both Nic and Ali, this has been the paperwork, particularly financial paperwork. As we committed to outsourcing this aspect of our businesses, we stepped into greater creativity. There were no longer feelings of regret, anxiety, and depletion in our businesses. Instead, there was creative flow because we could focus on the parts within the businesses that brought us joy, and we outsourced the rest.

If you are not actively creating ease in your life and business by expressing and living in your creativity, then you are reacting to the imbalance, resistance, and difficulty around you. If you take nothing from our book, please hear and digest this.

You are either in creation or reaction. You either create the life and business you desire, or you spend energy reacting to your life and business. We have both had plenty of years in reaction to life, and we spent most of our twenties living with the "Sunday night blues." Have you ever experienced this? It's the complete dread of Monday, the overwhelm and low energy that comes from anticipating the difficulty that comes when the workweek begins. At its peak, it was such debilitating anxiety for Nic that it even overtook half of her Sunday! Thankfully, we now show ourselves love and grace when we think back on these memories.

The truth is, you can't do better until you know better. Once you know better, you can begin to do better. This is why writing this book was so important. We are committed to sharing these techniques so that you can create a new reality for your entrepreneurial pursuits and your life.

One of the greatest techniques Nic uses to keep herself in creativity is taking her business out for coffee every Monday morning. Nic has practiced this every Monday for over fifteen years. In this meeting, she does a complete third-party, impartial, and unbiased analysis of how the last week in her business performed. She analyses what worked, what didn't, and what decisions and choices need to be made so that her inner creativity, her passion, and her happiness is maintained. It may sound arduous to some, however this simple act and commitment to creation enables Nic to stay ahead of her obstacles. This commitment allows her to anticipate solutions and problems before they occur; it enables her to know what to outsource and when, before the negative emotions of dread and overwhelm set in.

This technique is one that we teach all of the women we coach. We are serious about our businesses, and this technique is one that helps women take their businesses seriously.

Ali has implemented creation in her life by not getting stuck in the stories. Ali stays focused on the facts and on implementing solutions. By taking personal responsibility for her behaviour and any triggers she endures, she is creating the life she desires and not reacting to the life that she doesn't want.

Never take your profits, your brand positioning, or your stability for granted. At any time your business can be forced to change. This weekly meeting ensures you work on your business every week, not just in it. It can be challenging to find the time and mental space to work on your business in the monthly nine to five. Who are we kidding? In the early days of entrepreneurship, it is usually seven to seven! The point is you should always challenge yourself to work smarter, not harder. Work in and on your business at the same time. This, Monday morning coffee with your business creates breakthroughs, brings clarity of mind and allows you to look at the industry positions, your competitors, and your foundations. Please note that the internal barometer in this meeting is your feelings. As you step into analysis of all of the aspects of your business, allow your creativity and commitment to be in the forefront of all of your decision-making. As you do this, you will reach better flow, and you will steer away from feeding dinosaurs! You are your own million dollar formula, and you are your business. As you work on yourself and maintaining your creative alignment, you will experience wealth, health, and abundance like never before.

If you are reading this and saying to yourself, "I don't have time for a two-hour meeting every week," we challenge you do it just for a few weeks. We don't feel you can afford to not do it, especially if you are experiencing low vibrational and negative thoughts and feelings in your business. There is no better technique in this book with which to start.

This Monday meeting holds you accountable, and this may well be the beginning of an internal (and therefore external) transformation of your business. Once you have a few of these meetings, you may receive divine inspiration for a new direction, a new outlet of creativity that you had not considered. You may outsource, partner up, or see opportunities that were not there before. All of these are divine gifts and are the perfect next steps for you personally and professionally.

Now, let's talk about excuses. An excuse is something you tell yourself that stops you from taking action. As women, we often make excuses for ourselves from our negative mindset and belief patterns, as well as creating projections onto others. These two forms of excuse making are detrimental, however the latter is far more costly. Making an excuse internally from a limiting belief stops you from taking action. Projecting your excuse (such as using another person as your excuse) is very costly to your relationships and to your business.

To illustrate these two scenarios, let us give you examples.

Creating your own excuses. Fiona runs a bakery in Victoria and reached out to us. She had a viable business, however she was not making the profit that she had expected. This business was starting to create overwhelm, and her health deteriorated as the long hours and physical exertion took their toll. The limiting belief, in the form of an excuse that she was telling herself, was that she was not "clever enough" to be an entrepreneur. She had never excelled at school and had worked in hospitality for most of her life; this enabled her to have exceptional experience and know-how within her industry. When we spoke to her about how her experience actually stacked up to intelligence and know-how that could not be obtained in school, she connected with some inner worth that she had lost; she began to love and nurture herself. With our help, she began to realise that she did have the infinite potential to scale this business, and as she stepped away from this excuse, things began to change.

We encouraged her to connect with her creativity. What did she love about her bakery, and what had been her purpose four years earlier when she'd opened it? By using inner contemplation and applying Nic's technique of Monday morning meetings, she reconnected with her creativity, which was to create a beautiful environment where her community could connect and build relationships. Fiona is a gifted woman, and she is full of life and optimism; she's the life of the room and her bakery. Customers come from all around the region to connect with her and to experience her vigour. The more she connects and stays centred in her unique creativity, the more she smiles and is cheerful. She outsourced the tasks in her business she didn't enjoy. Next, she began to nourish her body and her soul with life-work balance, and she began to transform. Before our eyes, she became this effervescent woman who was limitless; she began to shine, and she even began to look different. She stepped up into creation within her life and her business. She is no longer stuck in an excuse she had on replay in her mind. She stepped up, claimed the space, and became her own million dollar formula.

Fiona stays committed to being in her creativity. Her business is growing, the numbers are climbing, and her business is becoming effortless.

Projecting your excuses. Holly had a soaring business importing furniture from the Middle East. She began this venture as a creative outlet while her youngest child finished high school. Never did she anticipate that it would grow, that her furnishings would be in demand, and that her life-work balance would be stretched to extremes. She had to be away from Australia two weeks out of every five.

When we met Holly, she was breathless. Nic remembers the first meeting. Even Holly's conversation was hurried; she was completely under the pump, and her ability to focus on Nic was compromised. Holly wasn't present because she was distracted with emails and phone calls. Watching her conduct her business was exhausting! She was a firefighter who leapt from crisis to crisis every hour of the day. She did her best to outsource, and her business continued to grow. Her greatest challenges were at home.

Holly was very angry at her husband. She felt let down by him, as if it was his fault she was so stressed. He was not maintaining the balance and well-being of their children, and as such their teenage daughter was having emotional and mental problems. She talked about him with a barb in her voice, as if every word was a hot poker being stabbed at him.

We were able to find her tipping point and get Holly to take personal responsibility for her life and business. Nic jumped straight in, lovingly asking her about her repetitive behaviours and the snarls that came out of her mouth. Nic asked about the love Holly had for her husband and her children; at this, Holly began to soften. Nic was able to find her tipping point, and the projection and blaming stopped. Nic coached her to take responsibility, be in a state of gratitude for her thriving business, and be in a place of empowerment with a plan to take to her daughter and her family. Together they worked for three months and recovered from all of the stress and anger.

Within three months, Holly was in her creativity, she loved her work even more, and her family and business flourished. When we started working with Holly, she was at the tipping point of damaging her relationships and her wealth. She was in the perfect place of imbalance, where her behaviour and her projection could have cost her the business or her family. She was making excuses left, right, and centre. She was completely out of control with nastiness and with volatility. None of this was who she is, what she was trying to create, or what she intended to do. This is what mental and emotional imbalance does. We taught her to stay centred and practise gratitude and mindfulness. We taught her about her creation process: if it's in your life, it's because you created it so, and therefore you are the only one who could fix it. It was not her husband's fault, and by admitting to her creation (although subconsciously), she then made her way forward into transformation. We are happy to say that her relationships continue to thrive, as does her business. She is present, is accountable, and steps up even more every day to her divine purpose and creativity. She claimed the space and became her own million dollar formula.

CHAPTER SYNOPSIS AND CALL TO ACTION

- Decide to love yourself consistently. This is your choice to make every day.

- Commit to a healthy mindset and step into your creativity.

- Work on your business and in your business equally, for greater success.

Questions to Ask Yourself :

Are you in reaction or creation in your life and business?

CHAPTER 2

Deciding to Trust Your Intuition and Take Action

When Nic was thirteen, she had a laminated picture on her wall that she'd bought from a gift shop. The memory is still there of asking her mother to drive to the gift store after school in the little town they lived in (Richards Bay, South Africa), where she'd purchased this picture. The picture was of a baby grand piano with roses lying on the lid, with the quote "God speaks always, but not always in words." Nic had seen this poster while she had been waiting for her mother to complete the grocery shopping the weekend before, and she could not get the quote out of her head.

Even today, she uses this quote with her coaching; something from the great depths of her knowing connected with these words. This picture was in her bedroom until she went to university, when it was packed up and placed into a keepsake box that is now sitting in Nic's parents shed. Through two moves to other countries and four bedrooms, this picture remained with Nic, filling her with the inspiration that connected her with the knowledge spoken to her from her soul.

God, Buddha, Allah, the universe, Christ consciousness, that incredible black woman in the clouds with wild and curly hair, the spirit of the sun—whatever it is that you are connected to, it is up there and always speaking to you. It is our understanding that this omnipotent source of love and creation, this vibration of this divine intelligence, is always trying to connect with us.

When we connect with it consciously, we are sure that the angels start applauding because they are always trying to work with us and support us. We call this divine being or energy that is up there the universe. God is always trying to speak to us—not just about the weather or packing the children's soccer boots, although the universe is great for those little reminders too. This universe loves you and is trying to get your attention and support you at every given moment. Messages of great love and affection, of encouragement and of divine guidance, are available to all of us at every given moment.

Nic understood this when she was thirteen. That little poster connected with some kind of memory and launched her into a life of prayer and service. She remembers being in prayer every day, a constant dialogue. At thirteen it was prayers for help with her math tests and the mean girls at school. As Nic grew up, the prayers changed and matured into asking for guidance about her life path, about wanting to live a life of service and make an impact on the world. These are the same prayers that she still prays every day. Nic has been fortunate and has had many incredible opportunities to be in divine service, such as building a school playground in Romania when she was sixteen and starting her own charity when she was twenty-four. By always searching for a greater connection, Nic is looking to create the change that she was placed here to do.

Later, when she was in university, she had a boyfriend who commented that she had the Midas touch, because everything she touched turned to gold. This was a comment about the financial abundance that was around her newly created business at the time—however, it was said with judgement and contempt, as if Nic had a special gift and he didn't.

We all have this gift every single moment of every day. It is the source of our hearts beating, and it is through grace that we have everything in our lives. The source is not selective;

the universe seeks us all, and we simply need to plug into the connection.

In Nic's late twenties, her dad commented that she must have some kind of fast-speed connection or direct phone line to God. He would joke, "How is your connection today?" The truth is the connection is always as strong and as fast as what you invest into it. The spirit is waiting for you to plug in the cable, pick up the phone, and start the dialogue.

Prayer is the fastest way to communicate to upstairs—prayers of gratitude, prayers for help, prayers for guidance, prayers of celebration. Nic's favourite prayer of all time is, "God, you rock!" She says this many hundreds of times every single day. The universe wants you to connect with it.

The truth is Nic doesn't have the Midas touch; she doesn't have any special gift. It has been a relationship of love and communication since she was thirteen. She had a few years of practice working together to materialise things in her life, and she received divine inspiration every day. Those are the guidance that show her in which directions to move. Nic thinks about her life as a big dot-to-dot puzzle, where she is holding the pen and the spirit is showing her which dot to move to next.

Ali has also experienced this connection, an inner knowingness that has always been there. It started with a connection to a Michael Jackson song. She would sing in the mirror with her pink hairbrush, "Heal the world and make it a better place." This song has become an undertone of commitment and drive for all she has gone on to achieve in her life. The spirit speaks, and Ali talks about this conversation as a universal nudge, an inner knowingness that a decision needs to be made, or a connection with someone that she pursued. For many years, Ali didn't trust this message that was delivered to her, or the universal nudge; instead, she would ignore it. As such, she would not pursue or reap the benefits of it. You are not crazy if you hear this little voice or have an inner radar going off. We all have this ability when we slow down, get quiet, and tune in. Ali uses meditation to stay plugged in to this connection and receive her universal nudges. This is a clear and consistent way to remain connected and listen when the spirit speaks.

These nudges do not always come as words, consider the picture on Nic's wall. They come as a knowingness or a little push or inkling. They can be a feeling or an annoying song on the radio. They can be repetitive words or a quote, a conversation, or a book on a shelf that is screaming for your attention. The universe speaks through any of the ways that you are willing to listen.

Nic had not spoken to her brother for a few weeks. Every day on the way to work for about five days, she had a feeling: "I should really call him and see how he's doing with the new project." Every day she put it off, or another phone call would come in on her way to work. Then one morning, on the way to meet Ali, the song "He's My Brother" came into her head. She said, "Okay, universe, I get it. I need to call him." Later that morning she called him, and they connected.

Have you ever experienced something like this? Little things like this happen every day, but our intellectual and conscious minds override the universal nudges. We brush them off and ignore them, and we think everything is a coincidence.

We know there are never any coincidences. When Ali and Nic met, it was not a coincidence. We met through community service, acting in a voluntary capacity on a board of a women's business network serving the region in which we lived. The process of us being on the board was synchronistic because Nic was nominated at the eleventh hour. We still continue to serve our community in this capacity, but deep down we know that the alignment for us being on the board was a deeper one: meeting each other. Nic remembers that a year before we met, other people in the community had said to her, "You should meet Ali V. You and her would really hit it off." Our paths had not yet crossed, even though we lived in a relatively small rural town.

Everything unfolds perfectly, and there is always a greater purpose and intent behind everything in your life. Stepping into this understanding enables you to work with this divine intelligence and, as Nic says, start playing the game of connect the dots.

The best news that comes from connecting the dots is we are not alone! You are not alone when you're suffering in your relationship that you are so desperately trying to turn around. You are not alone when flogging a business that is not yet in flight. You are not alone or unsupported in your suffering as you grieve for your father's passing. You are never alone. This divine support structure is limitless; it is in every particle of your being, every nook and cranny of your life. When you start communicating through prayer and gratitude, you start investing and building this relationship. When you have a relationship with whatever you believe is up there, it enables you to become more finely attuned to the messages and the universal nudges that are already around you.

What if we said to you that this innovative idea, this business, and your creativity is from up there? What if we said that if you started uttering the prayer, "Help me. This is a mess, and I can't see my way out of this," your life and your business would change? It is this simple.

> *Today, I will do what others won't, so tomorrow I can accomplish what others can't.*
>
> *—Jerry Rice*

The business that you are trying to develop or the innovative idea is divine inspiration. It is your divine purpose to take action on this inspiration and bring it to the world. We believe that in every sparkle of brilliance that comes into the world, the experimentation, the invention, and the innovative idea is given to several people on the planet. We all receive divine inspiration every day, and we often receive it as an idea or as a dream. Some of us get it like a lightning bolt in the middle of the night. This lightning bolt is delivered to several people on the planet at the same time, and the one who takes action and creates something with it receives the divine blessing and abundance.

When we close our hearts to the universe, we stop receiving the benefits of this incredible energy that is in the sky. When we are not open to receiving help, it cannot come flooding in. When we pray that prayer, we surrender some kind of ego-filled control that we have tricked ourselves into using, and the universe can finally step in.

Nic has been coaching this for years in her clinic, and she uses the following example. When you want the universe to come into your life, to show you incredible happiness in your relationships and financial freedom and incredible energy and health, what do you give up? It's like a five-thousand-piece jigsaw puzzle: you don't want to tackle this on your own; you want someone to sit down at the table and help you. It's overwhelming to start this puzzle on your own because the pieces are everywhere, and there are just so many of them! Similarly, the chaos in your life can seem overwhelming, and you don't want to do this alone. You want help, you want guidance, and you want to be shown how all the pieces fit together. But what do you let go of? When you pray for help, do you allow yourself to receive it? When you ask for help at the table, are you willing to put down all the pieces you have in your hand and let the other person share the load? Do you let people come in and help? The question is, do you let the spirit in and help? The universe needs to have access to the puzzle pieces in order to put them in place. Similarly, your friend helping you with the puzzle can't help you fix the puzzle without the pieces in your hand. This is a universal principal: you must be willing to hand over your burdens to the universe and then let go and be willing to receive.

It's like asking your husband to collect the kids from school but holding on to the car keys—it is never going to work! When you speak to the universe through prayer and gratitude, you must also invite them in. "I surrender. Your will be done here. I allow you into my life to shake things up according to divine will and according to the highest purpose of all involved."

You must give the universe the pieces of the puzzle if you are asking spirit to play and help you.

This universe we speak of is loving and full of grace. The universe is patient, and even when we are stuck in our suffering and are not ready to let go, it is there trying to get into the cracks of space that we have with divine wisdom and answers. This universe is forgiving and does not believe in punishment. Therefore we have to ask you what you are waiting for.

We have been there too, so stuck in the doing and in the process of being a mother, a wife, a daughter, and a sister. We were too busy being businesswomen that we forgot we had help available to us. We became fatigued, experienced burnout, and even regressed in our businesses and relationships while we learnt this very hard lesson. We are here to make a deep and fulfilling life for ourselves, and we are here to leave our mark on the planet, to imprint our brilliance and creativity on the lives of those around us. We are supported at all times. Perhaps it's time to step out of our own way and let in some assistance.

> *I stretch myself towards new success as I step into my ability to lovingly manage all aspects of my business.*

Nic experienced this eight years ago when she hit a wall in her business. She was running a thriving practice in Melbourne with a six-week waiting list, and this list situation did not shift for three consecutive years. Successful, one may think. On the outside it looked like the epitome of success. However, inside Nic was scrambled, overwhelmed, and exhausted. Trapped in the naivety of her twenties and caught up in the well-meaning opinions of others, she was pleasing everyone but herself. Her marriage fell apart because it was not being nurtured, and her health began to regress. Yet all the time, the phones kept ringing and the appointments were filled.

Nic reached entrepreneurial burnout. It looked like success on the outside because the dollars were flowing, and yet the truth behind the mask was one of fear and desperation. Nic reached deep into herself and into her connection with the universe. She plotted a path to regain her health and a healthy mindset, and to move her business into a new sustainable model that meant the waiting list disappeared. Nic now services over seven thousand patients per year, has a global business, and transforms the health of children and families all over the world. None of these divinely inspired ideas and the next chapter would have unfolded without the overwhelm and the sadness. There is a reason for everything!

We specialise in transforming the lives and businesses of women who are in positions like Nic was. There is a better way. Nic invested in mentoring, business coaching, strategic planning, and marketing education to develop the company Puraforce Remedies. Through this investment both within and without, she has stepped up to the divine purpose for which she was chosen. This divine purpose of bringing balance to women and families was not her intention when she ran her clinic in Burwood East. However, it is the legacy and the journey she has stepped up into that will leave an imprint on the planet long after she has left her body.

Ali had a similar experience, where suffering was indeed her transformation and her breakthrough. Ali was running marathons, running away from the emotion and the distress from a five-year infertility journey. She would run for three hours until the physical breaking point tipped, and then she could no longer run away from all the emotion. She would sob uncontrollably with grief and despair while her running buddies (all men) would hold the space for her. What a gift this time and running was for her. People can't keep it all locked inside, and this release of emotion was the beginning of Ali finding her solutions. After a diagnosis of coeliac disease and more emotional unpacking, she welcomed her beautiful twin boys into the world at thirty weeks. As one can imagine, the growth and the suffering did not end there, but they have equipped her to be at the point she needed to be. We are always exactly where we need to be. The suffering you are now experiencing is what will be the fuel for your rocket ships of success in the future. From your sufferings come your greatest learnings. We can shorten the length and duration of these sufferings if we slow down, get still, and listen. If Ali had listened to herself and to those universal nudges, instead of trying to run away from them, then perhaps her infertility journey may have been shorter. The past is the past, however these learnings have brought her to her place of service and understanding, and she now invests in the women we coach.

CHAPTER SYNOPSIS AND CALL TO ACTION:

- You are always where you are meant to be.

- From your greatest sufferings come your greatest learnings.

- To seek answers, get still, get silent, and listen.

Questions to Ask Yourself:

Are you listening to your universal nudges?

CHAPTER 3

Commit to What You Know

So what is the divine purpose for which you have been chosen? What is the business idea, invention, or innovation that you will bring to help stabilise the planet and restore Mother Nature to equilibrium and harmony? We promise you, it is already inside you.

What makes you heart sing? What brings you joy, and where do your natural talents and creativity shine? We encourage you to begin to step into this divine inspiration, plugging into this connection that we all have by spending time and conscious deliberation doing these things every day. As you engage your time in these things and channel your inner brilliance, your creativity, and your unique sparkle, you will begin to connect with your own million dollar formula!

As you meticulously create space for this inspiration in "the action hours," from 5:00-7:00 a.m. every day, you begin to walk in gratitude and receive divine inspiration and steps to begin the path to abundance and to the life you have been dreaming about. The success you deserve and can create is waiting for you to step up and claim it as yours, today and for all of the days here after.

Ali is one of those women others love to hate. She is good at everything, she is a lateral thinker, and she has the ability to commit to nutting something out until she has mastered it. She is one of four children and had many opportunities to work out solutions to problems herself. Watching her siblings and learning through doing has been one of the strengths she has taken from her childhood. As such, she has found herself in many different roles in her career, where she had to learn on the job and be creative in her solutions. For four years, she was in charge of turning around a firm that was $250,000 in deficit and yet maintain their competitive position in the market and community. Her abstract thinking is inspiring, however she has not always stepped up into the power of using this creativity.

Ali was a very high achiever at school, receiving the highest awards for academic excellence in high school. As such, there was enormous pressure placed on her to pursue academia at university, to which she rebelled. Ali is at her best and in her truth when she creates. She was talented in the arts and music and wanted to pursue a career in the arts. The pressure from teachers consumed her thoughts and led her to rebellion, which lasted several years after high school. Instead of applying her creative and academic talents, she slothed around and fell into opportunities. This time was not wasted, because people are always learning and growing. However, she could have used that time for a much higher output and personal expansion if she had been encouraged to pursue her dream. The story that this rebellion created for Ali in her life only ended last year, when she chose to face it head-on and commit to her creativity.

There is no better time than now to start living healthily.

Ali presented to Nic in her clinic as exhausted and overwhelmed. She could not maintain the demands of her international travel schedule, and her health was beginning to fail. She had manifested herself a neurological condition and had great pressure from her neurologist to be on epilepsy medication for the rest of her life, despite an inconclusive diagnosis. Nic challenged her about this creation in her life. What was the reason she had created these sabotaging symptoms? The symptoms built and became worse as she prepared to sing in front on 17,000 people in Las Vegas at a conference. It was an opportunity she wanted to pursue, and yet her health was sabotaging her.

Nic is very direct and cut straight to the point in their consultation. "You can continue to be in the story about you not being able to pursue your creativity, as you were told by your teachers in high school, or you can leave my clinic and make a more empowered choice to embrace your creativity and live your dream." Unbeknownst to Ali, these were the words she needed to hear that allowed her to give herself permission to pursue her creativity. Nic held the space, supported her body with Puraforce Remedies, adjusted her nutrition, and held her accountable to her empowered decision. Ali completely rocked Vegas! She was incredible, she was inspiring, and Nic cried as she watched the video. This was an inner transformation that gave space for Ali's health to completely resolve, and a new chapter of personal truth and expression began.

Ali now records her music once every three months in a recording studio, and she actively pursues creative projects in her business and community as a constant honouring of this divine gift of creativity. Ali's music inspires hundreds and has been a vehicle to raise community funds for passion projects in third-world countries.

What unique talent do you have, and what is the story you have attached to it? In what way could your life and your business expand if you stepped up and claimed the space to this aspect of yourself, which you currently keep hidden from the world? How long will you sit on this brilliance? Can we encourage you to give yourself permission right now? Could reading this book be your turning point, where you can love this side of you and incorporate it into your daily expression?

Personal freedom comes from giving yourself permission to be yourself at every moment of every day. You are your business, your business is your divine expression, and as such it needs to be the all-encompassing version of you, not just the versions of yourself that you are comfortable with the world experiencing.

VULNERABILITY IS THE KEY TO PERSONAL FREEDOM

Nic has struggled with vulnerability her whole life. Being an A-type personality and receiving criticism from peers in school for her achievements led her to shut down several parts of her unique expression. It wasn't until last year, with encouragement from Ali, that Nic began to tell friends and business acquaintances in her home town about her charity in India, www.rebalancetheglobe. org. Allowing ourselves to be vulnerable and at the mercy of the opinions of others can only occur when we are at a level of peace and acceptance from ourselves. Learning to truly love and back yourself all the time is a skill that often needs to be developed. As Entrepreneurial Babes, we mentor women in the process of learning to love and accept themselves.

At what point in your life did you stop backing yourself and start looking outside for external validation? Most of us have a story around this, an incident in childhood. Perhaps we felt embarrassed or ashamed, or there was a situation where we were unprepared or "not enough."

An example of a story Ali was stuck in was wetting her pants in front of Andy in year three in Ms. Fielke's class. This memory of being so embarrassed and ashamed had a huge impact on her. It inhibited her ability to get on stage and perform in front of people. There is still work to do on this as Ali stretches herself to greater levels of personal and professional performance.

One of the epidemics of our time is unworthiness. We meet this every day in almost every aspect of our lives. We constantly compare ourselves to others, and we look left and right to fit in. We are not born like this—we are born as unique creators, here to leave a unique sparkle and imprint on the planet.

Look inside yourself to connect to a story about worthiness that may be playing out. What actions, activities, and relationships are blurred with this grey shadow cast over them, where you feel you are not enough? The first affirmation we wrote together was our "Gratitude for Enough." This is such a powerful affirmation that rings to the core of each and every person we meet in our mentoring. You are enough, and you always have been enough. You need only turn on the light and see the magnificence of yourself. The world is ready for you to shine and leave your imprint.

GRATITUDE FOR ENOUGH AFFIRMATION

Thank you that I always have enough.

I always have enough confidence.

I always have enough talent.

I always have enough love.

I always have enough support.

I always have enough inspiration.

I always have enough nurturing.

I always have enough time.

I always have enough expertise.

I always have enough energy.

I always have enough creativity,

Because I *am* always enough.

We encourage you to work with this affirmation. Place an alarm every two hours and read this affirmation. Read it out loud, or even record yourself saying it. In this way, every two hours you have the opportunity to reprogram your thoughts and your consciousness with the reality that *you are enough*!

Nic had dreamed of being a writer. She was a great writer in high school, and her essays and articles were published in her late teens and during the first five years of her business. However, a program set off within her when she received criticism about an article that she had written. Rules specific to her industry meant that she was not able to truly write what her heart felt, and a barrier between her and her expression developed. It was several years before she began writing again for fear of criticism and exposure in her industry.

Nic undertook training in writing, and she read and listened to audio books about vulnerability. To write is to express thoughts and feelings, and to express ideas that are not of the mind but of the heart. To write is to act on inner expression and guidance that is bigger than you or me. As soon as Nic understood this concept, the vulnerability dissipated. Instead of writing for others, Nic began to write for herself. By writing for herself once again, she became connected to the inner feelings and thoughts that she had written about as a teenager.

The shift was one of embracing vulnerability. If your actions are driven by the approval or need of the good opinions of others, it is not an action from the self. It is an action driven by duty or the need to receive recognition or praise. This action is not heart centred and therefore cannot begin to be the expression of your personal truth.

Personal freedom comes when the vulnerability of being your true self and acting on your inner world begins, i.e., exertion without the consideration of external validation, praise and acknowledgement, truly expressing for expression's sake. This wonderful learning that came in the form of Nic's writing has taken her to the depths of personal pain about the vulnerability she had as a child, not just about her writing. Nic loved to dance and sing, but a program began around ten years of age that also created self-limitation in those areas.

To create and to be in creation is to express one's truth. To step and live one's truth is to do this consistently with courage and with an inner strength and knowingness that this expression is your divine inspiration and therefore needs no approval, validation, or approval from any other.

> *I just want to say, before I made this record I was doing everything to try and make my music heard. I tried to lose weight and I was making awful music, it was only until I started to be myself that the music started to flow and people started it listen. So thanks guys for accepting me for being just me.*
>
> *—Sam Smith*

Fear of embarrassment, fear of criticism, and fear of jealousy are some of the major limitations held by business people and entrepreneurs. We often unknowingly work out of this self-limiting programming, and limitations are placed on creativity and therefore business expressions. We see this time and time again in our mentoring: a story of self-limitation that creates a fear of vulnerability. From this fear of vulnerability, true creation and self-expression are not achieved, which limits the longevity and foundations of entrepreneurial pursuits.

Bringing your business to life and to market is actually bringing yourself to life and to market. As you explore the inner world of your creativity, you tap into your inner sparkle and expression that can and will flow into your business pursuits, and you consistently express this creativity to become your own million dollar formula. It takes immense courage and awareness to identify where your blocks and limitations are around vulnerability. As you commit to healing this place within yourself, you begin to access the miracles that are on the other side of the vulnerability.

Vulnerability is being demanded of the entrepreneurial person more now than ever before. With the emergence of social media platforms and the ability and desire to connect intimately with those with whom we do business with, vulnerability has come to the forefront. Resisting this vulnerability can be costly to your business because when you connect with the raw essence of yourself, you reveal your products and your service in a way that is highly attractive to the consumer. Nic experienced this when she blogged and opened up a YouTube channel for her personal stories and the application of her remedies. As she shares what her methods and lifestyle look like with her remedies, she engages new followers and consumers from all over the world.

This vulnerability has been a work in progress because she has dipped her toe into the big body of water that is social media. What is a level of vulnerability that Nic and her family can live with? You are your first million dollars, and personal branding is in the forefront of business people's successes. In many cases it takes a consistent pair of big-girl undies to take on the vulnerability within the social media platforms. The Internet and all of these platforms are permanent history, and so Nic has had to create some rules for the level of vulnerability she will show about her family. It is important for rules to be established with each social media strategy and campaign that you initiate in your business, because you truly are writing history with all that you place into this portal. You must ensure that the content you post will not hurt your family, yourself, or your brand in the years to come.

We mentor on this topic with all of our new businesses that require our assistance in the start-up phase. Your personal profiles are just as important as your branded and business profiles, because they hold the data and the following that will make or break your brand.

> *Your smile is your logo, your personality is your business card, how you leave others feeling after an experience with you becomes your trademark.*
>
> *—J. Danzie*

One of the major considerations within social media is alcohol and the values that are placed around this. Nic and Ali have strong values about the engagement of alcohol in alignment with business. There is nothing more unattractive than a businesswomen who is messy as a result of indulgence in alcohol. We mentor very strong boundaries around alcohol because every time that you leave the house, you are the representation of your business. This doesn't mean that you have to be in full hair, make-up, and stilettos, however it does mean that your attitude, opinions, and behaviours are always a reflection of your business.

It's important to take care that your comments are not seen as criticising other people or businesses, and also that your language is clean and professional. When you indulge in alcohol, the lines around the edges of your behaviour can become blurred. It's important that you step up to the plate consistently as the best version of your business is on show.

Ali remembers a situation when she was much younger and first out in the work force. Her language in a public place was inappropriate and colourful in the presence of her boss. This landed her in hot water, and she learnt very early about the boundaries required with alcohol and business.

The way we encourage our clients to do this is to ask about others and take interest in their stories. No one likes an EOE, or expert on everything. Learn to listen to others and what their needs are. You can learn a lot about your customers and your industry by listening to others. Only ever speak about your business in a positive context. Speak about how much you love your business; let people see the passion for your work ooze out of you. Refrain from talking about the struggles of business and how hard it is. Anyone in business knows that there are challenges, but if we are honest, that is part of the thrill. This is why we are entrepreneurs—we love problem solving! The conversation about how hard things are is for your mentors and your management team, not for the public or for family who do not know about your business. Sharing too much about your business may result in the public losing faith and confidence in your business as a result of your remarks.

With alcohol, hold yourself accountable to your decisions and your behaviour. Nic shares the story of how she went to the races one year and watched her accountant and his wife become very messy and unprofessional. Sure, they were having a good time, however Nic could not respect them the same way after what she had seen. You never know who is watching, and you are your business card and your million dollar formula. Your language, your dress code, your opinions, and your behaviours are reflections of your business and your personal brand. Therefore if you are going to celebrate with alcohol, do so at home. Do not allow yourself and your behaviour to be judged and cost you in your business.

Similarly, any posts on social media that hold any personal values or opinions can be used for or against your brand in the future. As the age of technology and personal branding continues to evolve, it may even be helpful to secure the domain names of all of your family, including your children. You never know what the future of entrepreneurship in your family may be, and you may want to secure a safe and untainted space for your children to develop a company in the future.

As an example of this, Nic and Ali have their personal Facebook profiles in direct alignment with their business profiles. We use social media mostly for entrepreneurial gain and networking rather than sharing large volumes of photos of our children and extended families. Making decisions about your level of vulnerability and the purpose of your personal social media platforms are important because at any time a customer or prospective business alignment can search your name and learn about you.

Do this exercise. Place your name into Google and see what comes up. See what comes up for your partner's name and for your children. These can affect your brand. We believe it is important to link your personal profile to your company and brand your personal page so that it has high respect and is representative of you professionally. Use these platforms for your business gain, not as a space to place unnecessary opinions which could potentially hurt you in the future.

As your business grows, so will you need to grow, and vulnerability is an inevitable step for those serious about personal and financial freedom. Striving for personal excellence in every aspect of your life requires you looking within with honesty that has not been pursued before and getting serious about releasing limiting beliefs and thought patterns that hold you back. Back yourself consistently and learn to be comfortable in the uncomfortable. Resisting emotional pain from your past regarding vulnerability is liberating and gives way for you to decide what your new experience will be. This need not be painful; instead, it can bring liberation that has not been able to pour into your life previously. Learning from your past enables you to release the story of being a victim of it. This empowers your ability to relate in a more human capacity, with more authenticity and the ability to show love and compassion to others. As you show yourself that compassion and self-love, you have the ability to lead your relationships in this similar light.

One of the greatest pieces of business advice that we share with people is that business is just a game. This may sound callous and masculine, however understanding this vital piece of the puzzle in the last five years has enabled us to access success and financial abundance like never before. If business is personal or becomes personal, it is because you have some unpacking to do. There is some personal baggage that is invading your business space, creating limiting thoughts and therefore limiting financial opportunities. If you have emotional triggers going off in your business world, or if you have limitations from these triggers affecting the relationships you have in your business life, it is time to take stock and personal responsibility to make some changes.

Your business can only grow as quickly as you are willing to grow emotionally. As you commit to stepping up, claiming the space, and being the best version of yourself, you will create meaningful, lasting, and honest business relationships. Your opportunity for personal and financial freedom will completely open up.

Life is one huge network of relationships. As soon as we conquer the relationship within ourselves to one of self-love, self-belief, and backing ourselves, we can do this to the relationships around us. As we show compassion, we can give compassion; as we show self-acceptance, we can accept others. This is no different in the business or corporate world; the same rules apply. Nourish your relationships and have integrity, love, and creativity flow through them. Treat others how you treat yourself: with reverence and with nurturing. Understand that there is a journey and a relationship of growth you are undertaking. Allow the relationship to be nourished, to make mistakes, and to reach peaks of infinite opportunity. This happens as we allow all of these things for ourselves.

Your life on the outside is the result of your inner world. If you have inner conflict and inner worthiness issues limiting thoughts and behavioural patterns, or if you have self-loathing and internal conflicts around abundance and wealth, so too will your outer world and relationships reflect this.

Get serious right now by nurturing your inner world to be right. By this we mean you should tend to your inner garden with love, light, and nourishment, and then your flowers on the outside will flourish!

We were serious when we established our partnership agreements in one of our businesses. We are very serious about our personal and professional success. We wrote a set of rules for our businesses and personal relationships. We hold ourselves accountable to this code of conduct regardless of where we are in the world and what we are achieving. These rules are in our office, and we hold each other to these rules as a commitment to each other and to our success.

Take our own advice and commit to personal and combined excellence at all times. Here are the rules we set out for ourselves.

1. No alcohol.
2. No politics.
3. No religion.

4. No children or husbands written or spoken about.
5. Nic to carry dental floss, toilet paper, and green tea bags for Ali at all times. (This prevents the distraction and meltdowns when she is unprepared!)
6. No phones to be used or checked when we are in creation.
7. Commit to the workflow established each month—no excuses!
8. Embrace our divine purpose in all aspects of personal and entrepreneurial pursuits.
9. No swearing on podcasts or live coaching calls. Our language is always a reflection of our business!
10. Give 100 per cent honesty and transparency about everything, all of the time! This includes our personal lives.
11. Give 100 per cent loving and supportive interaction and communication. Love is the foundation of our friendship and entrepreneurship.
12. No egos allowed! Love never has the need to be right or to be acknowledged. Loving communication allows no room for a fragile ego!
13. Continue to challenge each other by using *big* words. We are here for big transformation and to create big changes for ourselves and the planet. Use these words: substantial, considerable, huge, immense, enormous, extensive, tremendous, gigantic, mighty, momentous, monumental, epic, and mammoth!
14. No limitations, ever! Continue to dream big and support each other in our big goals and creativity.
15. Do not pursue anything that has resistance or difficulty. Only follow the flow.
16. Commit to effortlessness in all elements of our lives. Get out of the stories that create hard. Always follow universal nudges.
17. Own your stuff! Always accept personal responsibility for what is in your life. Be willing to change it and take action.

CHAPTER SYNOPSIS AND CALL TO ACTION

- Give yourself permission to pursue your creativity.

- Embracing vulnerability is the key to personal freedom.

- You are enough. Back yourself consistently.

Questions to Ask Yourself:

Are your behaviour, language, and attitude a reflection of your business that you wish to create?

Do not go past this first section of our book until you apply and conquer the learnings in this section. This will set you up for better success and greater benefit from all of our educational content.

GRATITUDE FOR

Enough

Thank you that I always have Enough.
I always have enough confidence,
I always have enough talent,
I always have enough love,
I always have enough support,
I always have enough inspiration,
I always have enough nurturing,
I always have enough time,
I always have enough expertise,
I always have enough energy,
I always have enough creativity,
because I am always Enough.

ENTREPRENEURIAL
BABES

PART TWO

Celebrate

CHAPTER 4

There Is Always Something to Celebrate

Nic didn't know how to celebrate. The #intensehippy was focused, in task and in consistent productivity for thirteen long years. She had not been taught to celebrate her successes; she had to be taught it was okay to stop and reflect on what she has already achieved. Every moment of every day of her life was governed by consistency and building on her success. Man, this was boring! Most of all, it was lonely.

Ali knows how to celebrate. She incorporates fun, laughter, and freedom into all that she does. This #laidbackprincess knew how to have fun but was easily distracted. Friends had bought her an egg timer to keep her on task and encourage her to focus and get productive.

Individually we were great, but together we are unstoppable. As we continue to collaborate, we are merging into this incredible business machine. We are reaching heights of success that we could not have achieved on our own. This beautiful collaboration and friendship has changed our lives, so much so that we made a commitment to ourselves and to one another to work together whenever we can. We share an office and step up to our creativity every morning in 'the action hours' at our office, or virtually if we are away on business. We celebrate each other's successes. We have a foundation of love, honesty, and accountability. We believe now is the time for women to begin supporting each other.

Unfortunately, as we reach greater heights of personal and business success, we also find ourselves open for more criticism, judgement, and jealousy. This was the reason that Nic had never celebrated her successes. Validating her success led to a vulnerability and an exposure that Nic had experienced as a child. There is a story there of being judged and criticised by her peers, and she had never visited this place again. These stories are so powerful, and we can cost ourselves so much happiness and potential as we remain stuck in them. As sad as we are to admit it, women are not generally supportive of other women, especially in the business and entrepreneurship arenas.

> *When others are up among the stars, celebrate with them. We were all sent here to shine, and we shine brighter when we all work together.*
>
> —*Unknown*

One of the values we share in our friendship is the ability to celebrate each other and for each other. We have the ability to not compare ourselves to each other, to never be in jealousy but to hold the space for each other's successes. We have spent time in discussions unpacking this core value of ours. What we shared was the loneliness and the sadness that had come from being in business alone and being open and at the mercy of the judgement of other women. It was and is very painful. From this we created our mission: to create a movement of friendship and success for businesswomen around the world, a place for women to celebrate each other and support each other on a loving foundation.

> *I am celebrating others' successes as if they are my own. As I do this, I create better success and opportunity for myself.*

Together we are pursuing a BHAG. Have you heard of this term yet? It's the new cool kids language. BHAG stands for "Big Hairy Audacious Goal." Our BHAG is to shape and establish Australia's upcoming leaders, teaching loving foundations and providing accountability for women to support and celebrate each other in business. We coach women to step up, claim the space, and be the best versions of themselves. We are stepping up to this goal with so much enthusiasm. The businesswomen and entrepreneurs we connect with are transforming themselves, their businesses, and their families' lives as they shape their communities!

Australia and the whole world over needs loving leaders who have vision and courage. Who better than women to step up, claim the space, and create governance and leadership that has higher morals, ethics, and integrity than ever before? However, this cannot begin to happen unless we abandon what has been done in the past. From our experience, women have been unloving, unkind, and cruel to each other. Instead of celebrating each other, we compete against each other. Instead of holding admiration, we hold jealousy. This needs to stop—now!

> *It takes a strong person to say sorry and an even stronger person to forgive.*
>
> *—Unknown*

Business and entrepreneurship is a challenging road requiring strength and courage that you didn't know you held when you first started. It requires leadership, vision, and support. The point is, this journey is hard enough without women around you making it harder! It's time for us to get off our soapboxes, stop putting each other down, and choose to support each other. It is a choice, and it requires growth and stepping outside of what you have done before. It takes turning your back on a behaviour that will come naturally. Choose to celebrate each other, not to tear each other down! When you step into this choice, you create for yourself a new level of personal freedom. You grow into a better leader and role model for your staff and your children.

This process of not tearing down others begins with you not tearing down yourself. What we have observed is that people who are hurt, hurt people in turn. The criticism and judgement you have about others is often the projection of your thoughts and feelings towards yourself. It is time to begin loving yourself and celebrating all that you are. The most powerful choice you can make today is to back yourself. You cannot wait for the approval of others. You cannot wait for your mother, your father, your spouse, or your girlfriends to get behind you. Liberate yourself! Commit to your BHAG and back yourself 100 per cent until you achieve it. Then repeat this process.

Now is your time to shine. You are only costing yourself your time and your success by looking outside of yourself. When we look outside ourselves for external validation, we are comparing ourselves. This is one of the most addictive and undermining behaviours we see in businesswomen. Make the decision to stop looking outside of yourself. You are enough, you always have been, and you always will be. What have you achieved so far in your life that is remarkable and deserving of celebration? We have many milestones in our lives that deserve celebration. This is not an egocentric undertaking; it is a process of self-validation and self-discovery.

Nic found this very confronting and struggled with this learning for several weeks. Nic founded her charity Rebalance the Globe in West Bengal when she was twenty-four. At the time she was alone apart from a few friends who assisted her with designing, marketing, and building a website. These pivotal months were tough as she faced enormous resistance and adversity in her undertakings. This struggle shaped her behaviour around the charity for the next eight years! Nic didn't share it with many people; she kept her achievements close to her chest because she was stuck in the story "no one wants to support a healthcare charity in India." This story, based on Nic's limiting beliefs, helped the charity in a place of steady growth but limited its expansion. It cost her charity greatly. When Nic met Ali, Ali really encouraged her to start speaking about her work and being proud of herself for what she had achieved. This was hard for Nic because she had to detach from the story and begin a new level of personal growth around vulnerability—if people know, then they could also judge. You may be reading this and wondering what you could possibly judge about charity work. There was judgement such as, "Why aren't you helping Australian charities?" and "You're just doing this as a tax write-off!" Both of these are not true, however the adversity and the challenge was real. If it's in your life, it's there to make you grow. Nic had to put on her big-girl panties and face up to the resistance. She had to be the change she wanted to see and commit to celebrating her own success, which meant digging deep and detaching from the opinions and criticisms of others.

Nic now shares her work, www.rebalancetheglobe.org, passionately and proudly. The truth is her company, www.puraforceremedies.com, funds this project, together with a few generous donations of individuals along the way. The truth always sets us free, and in Nic's instance, the truth was her charity, which has empowered and stretched her to the next level of personal development. She has once again had to step up and back herself and her endeavours. This is the greatest gift of all, and then the gift of job security for twenty-three staff and countless families' health being transformed through her charity work are the additional gifts that this personal development has enabled. In eight years, 145,000 people have had access to healthcare. The more Nic steps up and speaks about her work, the more support and opportunity she allows for the expansion and further development of her sustainable project.

So what are you hiding away from? What next level of personal development are you trying to wrangle your way out of? What in your life have you achieved that was outstanding and stellar, but you have not stopped to celebrate it? Now is the time to honour yourself.

A powerful exercise is to write out your journey so far. This is a great investment of time and energy. What has worked for you? Honour all you have done and celebrate your successes at the same time. Quantify for yourself your greatest learnings and analyse the decisions you have made. Have your decisions served you or cost you? As you look at your life in this reflective way, is there any love and forgiveness that needs to be undertaken towards yourself or others? Looking at your life under the microscope like this is confronting and requires great courage.

We are all the results of the bumps and the bruises in our life. We who embark on the road to entrepreneurship also have our fair share of bumps and bruises from the financial world. Do you become the mistakes of your past, or do you allow them to shape you? The difference between these two paths is your ability to disassociate yourself from the mistakes and see everything in your entrepreneurial life as an opportunity for growth.

When you do make mistakes, are you quick to anger, are you quick to blame others, and do you make it everyone else's error and mistake? This is an immature mindset. Instead, we must see every mistake as growth; that approach enables you to be a better person and better entrepreneur. Having this optimistic and more accountable mindset allows your mistakes and errors to glide over you and to freely flow in and out of your life. If you project your anger and the blame outwards, it becomes stuck and stays in your life until you learn from it. Any growth towards taking personal responsibility and changing your behaviour requires celebration. These stories are hard to get out of, because the programs often run really deep, back to childhood. Even undertaking this personal reflection and analysis, as well as your desire to create change, must be honoured and celebrated! You are amazing, and you are committed to personal excellence. This is a remarkable thing!

Taking personal responsibility for everything in your life and for what the mistakes and errors were, allows you to step into a self-loving mindset where change can occur. Consider such self-talk as, "Boy, what a creation! What can I learn here so that I don't need to create it again for myself in the future?" Forgiveness is an essential key to achieving this self-loving mindset with success. It is just as important to forgive ourselves when we make mistakes as it is to forgive others around us. Having this maturity in your business relationships allows quick transitions when errors do occur, and it definitely shapes you into an individual with whom people want to do business.

Ask yourself who you need to forgive. How can you display a more loving mindset to yourself and to the people within your entrepreneurial pursuits? Having this mindset is empowering and shows strength of mind and strength of character. Your personal success is directly related to your personal growth. Your business and your entrepreneurship are your individualised signatures of personal expression that you send out to the world. It may be packaged and gift-wrapped in an ice cream shop or an online shoe company, but it is still your individual identity and expression.

As you grow, not everyone in your life will grow with you. Sometimes as we grow, we can be targets for projected ideas, criticism, and limitations from others. As you grow and shake off these imposed limitations from others, you begin to install a foundation to your success. Knowing when to let go of other people's limiting ideas and beliefs of you, their criticism, and their negativity is crucial for your continued success. Investing and backing yourself 100 per cent of the time is essential to your personal and professional success. You can do this through honouring your successes and celebrating your milestones.

Decide right now that you will be your greatest advocate, that you do not define yourself by other's opinions, and that you consciously check out of the social commentary around you. We coach professionals who are limiting their own growth, successes, and income-earning capacity because they have decided to believe and invest in what others say and think about them. Through working with us, they identify where negativity and limitation come from, and they decide to stop the story. They then abandon these limitations and begin celebrating their successes.

We all have a story—every single one of us. Often these stories contain hurt and drama that will not serve us now or in the future. Consciously choosing to not engage in the story, to draw a line and step over it, and to leave the emotional baggage and pain behind can be all that is needed to stretch some of our clients to achieve the seven-figure income they desire.

Emotional limitations and beliefs in yourself reflect financial and lifestyle limitations. How much are you costing yourself right now because you continue to live in your story? Put the story to bed; decide now to step into your best expression of yourself and your business. Commit to celebrating yourself because you are a rock star. You are unique, are powerful, and have limitless potential. When you choose to back yourself, you are going to achieve incredible things!

CHAPTER SYNOPSIS AND CALL TO ACTION

- Consciously celebrate all of your successes. Write down everything you have achieved in your life to this point, and have a celebration. You are amazing!

- Disassociate from others' judgements, criticisms and social commentary about your life.

- Back yourself 100 per cent of the time.

Questions to Ask Yourself:

Have you given yourself permission to let your light shine?

CHAPTER 5

Knowing When and How to Change

In life and business, change is both essential and inevitable. Change can be viewed as challenging or frightening for many of us. Others see it as another task on their to-do lists, as something they have to endure. What is your attitude to change? Success is knowing when to change. Success is being in balance with the now and the future, and bringing forth learning and experience from the past. In business, being able to straddle this horse of the now and the future is a skill that requires strength and great confidence; it's a unique skill in which you manage your emotions and materialise your dreams.

Change is a good thing. It always represents a change in a better direction or a new opportunity for even greater abundance and growth. Many people resist change and create for themselves incredible resistance and emotional pain when there are changes in their lives. Being able to ride the changes in your life is courageous, but it is as important as getting sleep and drinking water. The only permanent thing in life is change, and so the sooner that we embrace it and learn to work with the inevitable, the easier the ride will be.

I am willing to embrace change.

Embracing change is a mindset; it is an attitude and a choice to being open to something that is even better for you. It is similar to trying a new food in a restaurant, it is an opportunity to experience something delicious and enjoyable. Like all aspects of your personal development and business success, change is directly linked to the attitudes and choices you create for it.

We have said it already: your business is a direct expression of your mindset and personal development. Similarly, change is a wonderful barometer to highlight the resistance you still have within you for personal growth. Viewing change as an opportunity to grow and to experience better things in your life is a healthy attitude, whereas negativity, complaining, and begrudging change is an attitude that assures the change is going to involve blocks and obstacles.

Like every day of momentum and progress you have had in your business, it started from a thought that manifested as a choice. What is your choice about change? Are you choosing to embrace the new and the continual opportunities that you are creating for yourself, or do you choose to swim against the tide and make the change have drama, expense, and depletion for you as you resist the inevitable?

We challenge you to contemplate what your thoughts and beliefs are about change. Perhaps now is a time to re-examine your attitude and make a different choice. What we know for sure is when you make the decision that change is going to bring incredible gifts of happiness and abundance in your life, you close the door on pain and stagnation in your life and your business.

> *The secret of change is to focus all your energy*
> *not on fighting the old, but on building the new.*

> —*Socrates*

As you embrace the new you, you find happiness and fulfilment, just like Nic stepping out of her comfort zone and stepping into fun and celebration. Before our collaboration, Nic didn't do friendship and Ali didn't do partnership. Stories and self-limiting beliefs about being hurt, financial ruin, and conflict were at the base of these limiting decisions we had made for our lives. We both had some unpacking to do. We both needed to do personal work, let go, and forgive. We also had to celebrate all we had achieved individually and then step into the next level of success, backing ourselves in the unknown and in the challenge of a friendship and a partnership. We are so happy, we are productive, we are passionate, and we have so much fun! On the other side of letting go of these stories and celebrating your success is even greater happiness and opportunity.

In order to create positive change, you need to know what success looks like. What is success to you? There is no point in starting to run if you don't have an idea of the race in which you are competing. We all define success differently and step into entrepreneurship with different motivators. Some of us are driven by money, others are driven by people; some are driven by lifestyle, freedom, and opportunity. None of these are wrong; they are simply different. What success are you chasing? Is it to own a personal aircraft, to have family holidays, to create financial security for your family? How do you measure your success along the way?

Ali is good at almost everything, and she has always been a very good goal setter. She has always been able to articulate her small goals and achieve them, and therefore there have been lots of celebrations at the end of each milestone. Nic is better at the long-term, big-picture goals; as such, they take longer to achieve, and there has been disregard of the progress that is made every month and quarter. We are also motivated by different things. Ali is motivated by praise; Nic is motivated by productivity. To make Ali feel validated and supported, Nic needs to give her positive feedback and encouragement. For Nic to feel validated, her agendas and tasks need to be completed. Understanding these different currencies and leverage has been powerful in our ability to work together and celebrate each other.

Nic comes from a family of very high achievers; her parents and her brother have done very well in their lives, and they have great success and happiness. They have created wonderful security for themselves and as such have been able to show great charity and give back to the world. Therefore with a baseline of such height, Nic was very critical of herself. She never felt that she was enough and would constantly insist that she could do better. In reality, the success that she was driven by had no comparison to that of her family; what drives her is the ability to change lives and have an information exchange about healthcare. Understanding that this was her true measure of success stopped her self-sabotaging thoughts and behaviours. This allowed her to step into celebrations every month, looking at all of the people whose health has transformed as a result of Puraforce Remedies.

How are you measuring your success? Is it being measured by your true purpose and intent, or are you giving your personal power and celebrations away as you set your goals and your milestones on the values of others? What are your core values? What does your business, your personal brand, and your life mean? What are you here to create, what imprint will you leave and what is most important to you? Core values include things like integrity, generosity, happiness, freedom, peace, and social accountability.

Each year over the Christmas holidays, Nic does an evaluation on her businesses and her charity. She revisits her core values to ensure they continue to align with creativity. When you undertake personal development and self-discovery, you step into a world of rapid growth. As such, your business interests may need to adapt and be adjusted as your values change. If they don't change, this is okay, however revisiting them once a year enables greater accountability for yourself and the opportunity to celebrate the success you have created around these core values.

At the core of Ali's success is her fun-loving nature. The honest truth is that Ali will not get the job done if it's not fun, because one of her core values is to have fun. Once she identified this core value of hers, she was able to shape all of the tasks in her life to be more fun, and she became more productive. She wants to do more that is fun, and so by default she gets more done. What is a core value of yours that, if you reshaped it, would bring greater rewards and productivity?

We pull businesses apart that are not functional and profitable and put them back together with specific strategic plans, vision, wealth, and growth mapping. We do this by addressing and drawing out the core values of the business owner. Some of you may think this process is arduous, but we believe it is essential. If you do not have an idea of what success is to you, how you will measure it and continue to create it? Otherwise you are looking for treasure without a map, just floating at sea. There can be no joy and celebration if there are no parameters or targets in place. These fundamentals ensure there are celebrations and joy along the way. Business is fun; it is a game of complexity and skill. It is an undertaking for the driven and the inspired, not for the naive and the boring.

What comes out of your mouth is just as important as what rolls around in your head. The language you use about your life has a great impact on your happiness and your outcomes. As you speak, you breathe life or death into your business. People who speak of business as hard, impossible, and gruelling get this experience in their business. We are far more cautious of the language we use because we desire fun, laughter, ease, peace, and effortlessness. What if success and opportunity could be all these things? We can tell you it is! When you speak these languages over your life, over your relationships, and over your business, you begin to see miracles and changes before your eyes. We do our best to hold each other accountable to using words such as "challenging" instead of "problems." We use positive statements with laughter, such as, "Boy, this is what success looks like! It's really stretching me to new levels of self-empowerment!"

When you accept and take personal responsibility for the language you use about your undertakings, you begin to realise how many times you complain and resist the grace and ease of business. Every word out of your mouth is a message to the universe. Unfortunately, the universe doesn't have a filter; it is a feedback system that bounces back to you like a ping pong ball you hit across the table. What are you putting out there?

Do your best to eliminate these words from your vocabulary entirely: hard, tired, overwhelmed, stressed, impossible, terrible, miserable, incompetent, horrendous, stuck, and difficult. Also, try eliminating the word "try" from your life. You are either doing it or not. You are either backing yourself fully and committing to be the best version of yourself in personal excellence, or you are not. There is no trying! You can't try to create wealth—you are either creating wealth or not. Instead, speak words of life into your business.

> *Every day, I commit to being the best version of myself, which guarantees my personal and professional success.*

Your language is also a reflection of your business and who you are. If you are negotiating a contract, building a relationship, or trying to empower staff, dropping swear words will not bring you respect or assist you in building your relationships. Climbing to the top requires the correct behaviour.

Ali has a lot of experience in networking. Nic needed coaching and refinement to adjust her behaviour while attending long, drawn out evening events. Nic would do really well holding herself gracefully, even if she was in pain, however once it hit 9:00 p.m., she was always ready to call a cab. This behaviour and opting out was damaging to her business. She didn't have the opportunity to connect with everyone she wanted, or to leave her mark on the event. Instead, she would bail because she was tired. We remember a drive home from an event in Melbourne, where Ali lovingly held Nic accountable for her behaviour. She was not being rude, obtrusive, or awkward, however we had spent a lot of money getting to and from the event, and because of Nic's impatience and attitude, we did not get everything out of the opportunity that we had hoped. This was a valuable lesson for Nic, and she has stepped up and claimed the space in the months since. You can't do better until you know better. Nic had practiced in a clinic alone, and she had mastered the clinical relationship. Her business had expanded and thrived for so long that she never needed to build relationships with others in her industry. She was self-sufficient with her chosen professionals to support her, such as her accountant and financial planner, and as such she had never played the networking game. Similarly, she had never nominated herself for any awards or attended any VIP or glamour events; this was simply not part of her success at that time. When we started working together, this soon changed. Ali encouraged Nic to become comfortable in the uncomfortable. She was required to step up, claim the space, and grow to the best version of herself in these new social situations. She was challenged to get comfortable in wedges, lipstick, and more hairspray than she'd ever used before.

Some of you may be reading this and thinking, "Hang on. This isn't genuine. Nic is not being herself." You know what she was? She was growing and adapting as her entrepreneurial life required. In the same way that personal and deep belief systems need to be challenged, so did her ideals about make-up and jewellery. Business requires you to become comfortable in the uncomfortable. Sometimes we have to go outside of our comfort zones, and we have to stretch ourselves and upscale to become better. For Nic, this was learning about social etiquette, mastering the art of small talk, and being able to nail her elevator speech of who we are and what we stand for two hundred times in one night. It is all growth, which means it is all positive!

For some, it is learning to be comfortable in front of an audience. Many people come to us and ask how we have developed great public presentations. We present in front of thousands of people each year, and we do it effortlessly. However, just like Nic and her first time in heels, it's not always elegant or easy. These are necessary steps to your success.

We encourage you to stop meeting this growth with resistance. Stop the dialogue, drama, and negativity around this growth. Step up and claim the space! Enrol yourself in Toast Masters, employ a presentation coach, and make commitments and decisions to master every one of these skills. As these aspects become the extension of your business card, they become your million dollar formula. Every step that you make towards personal excellence sets you up for even greater opportunity and wealth generation.

Nic can now walk into a room with confidence. She can sit through a long and tedious dinner with grace and respect, and no one on the outside would know how bored and frustrated she is at the lack of punctuality and professionalism during the event. Why? Because her business behaviour has improved. She has held herself accountable to being her best at every moment, whether she is coaching, in meetings, managing staff, or even writing this book.

The commitment to personal excellence makes you a better human being. It makes you a better mother, wife, friend, daughter, sister, and entrepreneur. Wanting to stretch and grow, better yourself, and serve your community are wonderful goals. We believe every entrepreneur shares this goal; they want to be the best they can and leave an imprint on the planet. Your business does not need to be global, your turnover doesn't need to be enormous, and you don't have to be the biggest and best to make a difference. By honouring that inner voice, that purpose and creativity inside of you, you can make a difference.

Each of us has a role to play, however we are destined to work in collaboration. At the basis of all business, in every language, industry, and continent, is the same thing: relationships. If you cannot connect with people, you cannot build rapport; if you cannot gain and maintain trust, this game of business is going to become difficult for you. Accepting the importance of improving interpersonal relationship skills, building connections, and being able to network are essential for entrepreneurial mastery.

Ask yourself what your business behaviour is. Are you quick to become restless? Do you have negative comments about other businesses or industries and your competitors? Do you have the capacity to maintain healthy relationships in your workplace, or are you quick to anger and slow to forgive? Be honest with yourself and then begin to improve.

How is your language? Nic has a chuckle because she spent most of her life living overseas. However, when she returned home to Australia, she was based in Victoria. When she moved for a tree change to Mount Gambier, South Australia, she noticed there was a tendency for South Australians to say "somethink" instead of "something." Many business professionals do this too. It came to Nic's attention when we began recording our Entrepreneurial Babes Podcast Series. We were in the studio recording, and Ali dropped a "somethink" into the recording. We laughed it off, however Ali has held herself accountable ever since, and if you listen to the podcasts, you will hear Ali correcting herself if she makes this error.

Personal excellence is one of the greatest commitments you can make as an entrepreneur. Celebrate where you have come from and then build on this as the new foundation for your success. We are very passionate about health and well-being. We coach people who are at the tipping point of adrenal fatigue and entrepreneurial burnout, and both of us have been there ourselves.

You are your own business card, and so your health and well-being becomes essential to the sustainability and longevity of your business. Without solid foundations, you do not have the ability to extend yourself and your business. We coach people about the essentials of hydration, nutrition, exercise, sleep, and practicing mindfulness. We advocate three litres of water every day, as well as eating a high-nutrient diet full of vegetables, fruit, and lean meats. We advocate twenty to forty-five minutes of exercise every day, and we balance this throughout the week with intense and gentle exercise such as walking, yoga, cycling, and weight-bearing exercises. We encourage three mindfulness practices that we implement in our daily lives. Begin your day with meditation, gratitude, and manifestation. Every morning in "the action hours," write down three things you are grateful for and three things you are trying to manifest. Every two hours throughout the day, set the alarm on your phone and read aloud or listen to the recording of "Gratitude for Enough Affirmation." Finally, practice five to ten minutes of silence and reflection in the evening before you go to sleep and revisit the gratitude and intentions you set in the morning. You will be amazed at how this solid foundation enables you to maintain your personal excellence when it comes to energy and performance within all aspects of your life. We practice this every day, regardless of where we are in the world and what is on our calendar and in our inbox.

> *As I surrender my ego and step into love, I can be*
> *of service to myself and others.*

One of the most admirable qualities in a successful entrepreneur is humility. At the same time that we encourage you to celebrate your successes, it is important to abandon your ego as you climb to higher levels of personal and professional success.

One of the greatest gifts that comes along with entrepreneurial success is personal and financial freedom. This is where true fun and creativity can be expressed because you have choices and flexibility about how your time is spent. You get to choose what projects you spend your energy on, and you can facilitate multiple income streams. This is when collaboration and interpersonal skills are often tested the most; we can get stuck in the "right way" of doing something simply because it's the way that we have done it before.

Being able to work with others successfully requires disconnection from the ego. Learning and mastering the act of being humble is essential to success. We have all met people who are dominant and powerful and have achieved great things. However, no one wants to work with them because they are so rigid. These people are locked in their way of doing things, can become aggressive, and are not open to receiving feedback or instruction.

Nic often says to Ali, "If I get like this, take me outside and hose me down with cold water!" There is no room for delusions of grandeur, there is no room for ego, and there is no room for bruised emotions in the game of business. If you are in business, it is your top priority to get along with people! It is your business to be slow to anger, to be quick to forgive, and to be quick to empower others to create their own solutions.

As your business scales, you can cost yourself greatly if you have an ego or cannot surrender control. We mentored Judy, who was a powerful and successful woman who ran a financial planning consultancy business in Sydney. She was a stellar networker and could work the room, but once people began to peel back the exterior, she was ice cold. We experienced this first-hand in a few phone conversations before she met with us to begin her coaching.

The truth was her communication via email and phone was fierce and to the point, but it was really cold. Her language was punchy and efficient, which was great, however her ability to build relationships was poor. You needed to be a tolerant and understanding person to see past her business behaviour, and she was quickly making enemies in her industry! She was a woman and successful, which already made her a threat in her industry, however her tongue had become stronger because she felt overwhelmed in her business. The truth was she was great at the numbers. Her advice made people happy, but she was a pain to deal with.

To be honest, we found her intimidating, however our job was to create some reform and change the biggest issue in her business, which was her communication. She was losing staff, and her office was not a pleasant place to be. There were raised voices, and her business behaviour left much to be desired. Judy had some personal growth to do.

When we began to challenge her behaviour and explain its cost to her business, as we expected it was met with fierce resistance. However, underneath it was a massive ego. You see, Judy had done very well doing it her way. She had salvaged her business from a volatile merger a few years earlier, and she had worked around the clock to deliver results to her clients. She transformed their portfolios and made a lot of people happy. This was the backbone and success of her business.

We encouraged her to celebrate this and to re-evaluate the direction and the intention behind her company. What was she doing it for now that she had created personal and professional freedom for herself? What was she motivated by?

In a two-hour coaching session, we managed to extract her inner essence underneath that big ego! Her passion was to empower young professionals with large incomes to invest their money rather than (in her terms) "piss the money up the wall." She spoke of the young medical professionals who made up a lot of her business and did not manage their money correctly. She spoke of the immaturity these young people had and how they did not realise that with such large salaries, they could achieve so much. We'd found her passion, and now she had to transform it into the foundation of her new business behaviour and expression.

We worked with Judy over a few months, and over time the ego deflated. After seeing the costs to her business, Judy realised she had no choice but to change. We had to wear our big-girl panties into those first few meetings because Judy really was a force to be reckoned with. We coached her about articulate language, active listening, and the importance of empowering her staff with the permission to have their own ideas. Over a few months, the business really changed. Her staff began to respect her, her office was a lovely place to be, and she was no longer overwhelmed.

You don't know what you don't know, until you know. We had to lovingly hold Judy accountable for her business behaviour, her temperament, her language, and her inflexibility. Once we had pointed it out to Judy, she knew better, and she could do better. This was the beginning of the transformation.

As you can see in Judy's story, there is no place for ego or judgement. This is an obvious story, however sometimes we work with people whose egos are not so big and easy to see. Sometimes ego can be disguised as control. We all know control freaks, but what about the hardcore ones who are inflexible and controlling in business? Have you worked with these people? We sure have! These people who are control freaks on the outside are often paralysed with fear of failure and have low self-worth. This is often the foundation of their behaviour. Showing these women kindness and loving interaction instead of butting heads with them is often all they need to soften. These women are often quite passive in their intimate relationships, however they run a tight ship in the home. They often have homes that look like museums, they cannot manage clutter or mess, and they require order as the centre of their mental and emotional clarity.

Send these people love, because these women don't know any better. Their behaviour is often a coping mechanism because they are so fearful of being wrong or making a mistake. The ego comes across as inflexibility and perfection. These women often cannot handle change and require processing time. Learning to manage their anxiety and behaviour can be the key to success. Give them plenty of notice if change is required, stick to their agendas and deadlines, and enforce personal development as part of their roles.

We have managed many people like this over the years, and we show grace and laughter when they make mistakes, teaching them that they are allowed to be human. These people are often exhausting to be around because they are a bundle of nerves, are short-tempered and irritable, and are pathologically early. These people are dynamite for your business because they get stuff done! You simply need to manage their fragile egos and ensure they don't implode under their self-imposed pressure. Active encouragement and celebrating their successes can help strip down their egos and build up their self-confidence. Little gifts and cards of encouragement go a long way with people like this!

Remaining human, relatable, and humble despite your position, your bank balance, and your age is essential in business. We like to think of it as people in business going home and still having to clean up their children's vomit when they are sick. Nothing is ever beneath us: we still vacuum our floors when the children make a mess, we still shop for our groceries, and we have to wait in line at the supermarket.

Never allow your ego or your success to cost you your business, your friendships, or your opportunities. In business, we all want to work with people who are warm, grounded, realistic, and honest. Focusing on being the best person you can be and modelling your business behaviour on the kind of woman you would like to do business with sets you up for great success.

Be a person of your word. If you say you are going to do something, then follow through and do it. Similarly, if it doesn't interest you, you don't have time, or you don't want to make space for it in your life and business, then don't. Be honest in your communication with people so that you set up your relationships for success. Be proactive in your relationships, explain your feelings, and state your positions and intentions early in the piece so that the relationship can move forward.

Most important, have integrity. In everything you do, make sure that you never take advantage of someone else and that your decisions and actions do not hurt another. Having this high level of ideals and stating this as part of your business values makes you attractive to do business with or work for.

We live in a time where employees demand more from their employers than ever before. They require being kept in the loop, respect, and reciprocation, and in many instances they demand social responsibility from the companies for which they work. Employees want to be part of your vision; they want in and have feelings of fulfilment. Deep down, every human wants to feel valued, honoured, and part of something bigger than herself.

After the global financial crisis of 2007-2008, entrepreneurship changed. Before the crisis, wealth was about dollars and cents. There were several big key players, and they had massive deep pockets that had little impact on others or brought any positive contributions to the planet.

Once the crisis hit, it became a bit more of an even ground. The world changed, and the platform shifted to a place where each entrepreneur had a better opportunity to have a piece of the pie. Wealth changed from wealth for wealth's sake to wealth with impact. Social entrepreneurship, social and ethic investments, and collaboration were achieved like never before. As the years passed, this trend has continued, and as consumers we have demanded more from industry and companies than ever before. We have adjusted our spending to have more of a mental and emotional lean than just financial value.

Businesses are being held to their promises, and their greater impacts. We feel this is a great move forward because we are committed to creating change with our wealth. With wealth comes an opportunity to make different choices and contributions to change the lives of others. However, without personal credibility from following through on what you say and your promise, there is no foundation. Women often have great intentions, and they are quick to articulate them. Once this is heard by others, it becomes a promise. If it is not upheld or doesn't come to fruition, the result can be damaging.

Ali was an example of this. For twelve months she had told others in her professional circles that she was writing a book. This was her intention, however she had to plan to bring it to fruition and create this reality. Ali wasn't lying, but this premature announcement without a plan could have been damaging to her networks. Nic challenged her on this and encouraged her to stop telling people about the book. When Nic held her accountable and asked her how and when, she had no answers; the truth was it was only in inception, and she was early on in the creative process.

Nic turned this into action with a plan. We added it into our workflow and made it a reality. Once the manuscript was near completion, we began to speak about it. We breathed life through our language by building anticipation and excitement about the book with full purpose and understanding of how it was reaching completion.

The message here is that you shouldn't open your mouth unless you can back it up or know that it will be delivered. If you are unsure, then be honest and state that you are unsure about how you are going to complete something.

Nic displays these skills for one of the boards on which she serves. She has a monthly commitment to the board and has a portfolio she manages. Before she took on the position, she was clear to the chair about her ability and time commitments in the next twelve months. From then, it was decided that Nic was still of value to the organisation, and she could perform and be accountable for what she had communicated. Therefore there is no resentment, disappointment, or resistance when she says no to taking on additional tasks or responsibilities.

We only have twenty-four hours in the day, and in business we meet people we want to work with all the time. Being transparent and honest in your communication about your interest and timelines makes for a better and more transparent foundation in your collaboration.

> *As I step into the space of following through with my commitments and intentions, I receive respect and credibility.*

Your credibility and integrity are the signs of your success. What others say about you as a business person is important because these words build your brand and your reputation. We make our interactions in business as flawless as possible. A lot of preparation and intent is spent working on our businesses and building credibility. We work *on* our businesses more than we do *in* them, building on the foundations of our success.

Ask yourself how others experience you in business. If you are brave enough, perhaps even ask your staff and your team five questions; be open to receiving feedback. Nic asks Ali for feedback after every seminar, presentation, and mentoring session we have. This is a commitment to personal excellence. We can always improve, and a willingness to continue to learn, grow, and be challenged keeps your ego in its box. Be willing to receive constructive feedback, and be humble enough to admit when you make an error. Do not be afraid to say you don't know—never try and bluff your way through. Not only will you fail publicly and lose the opportunity, but you will also create damage for your reputation and brand.

Ali set herself a challenge in her business. She told her team, "Tell me something you like about my leadership. Is there anything I can improve on?" Not only was she brave enough to ask for the feedback, but she was brave enough to receive the answers. Data doesn't lie. The results came back, and she had many things to celebrate in her leadership. She also has made a commitment to personal excellence and is making an effort to improve in the areas that were shown to her. One area of feedback was that Ali always looked distracted when she was at conferences. She has now set some rules about her behaviour, which enables her to be less distracted. Ali now makes a concerted effort to be present in the now. We are all works in progress.

Nic and Ali have set rules around their business behaviour. When people associate with us in business,

1. We are punctual.
2. We are professional.
3. We never comment negatively about other companies or industries.
4. We always speak with an emphasis on positivity and enthusiasm.
5. We are slow to anger and eager to forgive.
6. We never drink alcohol—ever!
7. We never put ourselves down. We are the best we can be, so there is no place for self-criticism and put-downs.
8. We always ask for help and admit when we do not understand or need further information.
9. We own our stuff, and we never project our personal opinions unless they are asked for.
10. We never commit to doing something we have no intention of completing or being involved in.
11. We insist that honesty is the only policy!

Always behave in the way you wish to be remembered. You are your business card!

A wonderful task that we encourage you to complete is to write out your life and business journey so far. What have your stories been? What are your limiting beliefs, and what have you learned along the way? Then burn it! Once it is burnt, sit and reflect. Understand that by doing this, you have drawn a line in the sand. You now have the opportunity to create something different. This exercise is very powerful and is great to do at the end of every month. What has the month been like? What will you do differently, and what can you improve on?

This cathartic burning can also be used when you need to release something mental or emotional, or you have some challenge or obstacle that you cannot seem to move past. Many entrepreneurs struggle to turn off; their family time can be consumed with their work, and they can struggle to relax and detach. Writing and burning is a form of surrender. We often use it when we come up against resistance that we can't seem to move past.

Take the time every Sunday night to write about the week you wish to create for yourself. Include words like ease, effortless, peace, joy, abundance, exponential growth, limitless, and joyful. This is a great habit to adopt that keeps you in creativity and setting intentional purpose and energy into your week. Here is an example of what this exercise looks like.

> I'm so happy and grateful now that I am living a life of personal and financial freedom. With every day that passes in my life and business, I am growing and becoming a better leader and entrepreneur. My reputation and efforts are being honoured and acknowledged by others, and I have industry leaders and other global opportunities coming my way all the time. My income is not only secure but is growing exponentially. My potential for growth is limitless as I align and collaborate with others,

creating for myself further abundance, financial opportunities, and income diversity. My future is safe and secure. I have systems and structures in place that support the sustainable growth of my business. I have no problems in my life, only opportunities for me to develop and grow into a better person.

I have a peaceful life, and I do not attract drama or chaos. I have no suffering in my life. I am blissful, content, and living the life of my dreams. Every day I step into my creativity expressing my divine purpose, and my success is effortless.

CHAPTER SYNOPSIS AND CALL TO ACTION

- Put your ego back in its box. There is no place for ego in business.

- Strive for personal excellence, be open to feedback, and then make improvements.

- Be flexible and open to change because it's the only thing that is ever constant.

Questions to Ask Yourself:

Can you surrender control? Are you willing to collaborate with others?

CHAPTER 6

Speak Abundance and Ease into Your Future

When you close your eyes and dream about your future, what does it look like? If you were to paint a picture, write a book, or run a marathon, can you picture yourself doing it? When you close your eyes, can you visualise yourself achieving it? Feeling how elated, satisfied, fulfilled, and joyful you would be when you achieve your dream is an important part of the manifesting process.

You must be able to feel in your heart and your spirit the feelings of success and achievement. Manifestation is a three-step process.

1. You must know with clarity and intimate details what you are trying to manifest into your life.
2. You must close your eyes and feel the joy and gratitude that comes from the knowingness that you have achieved your goal.
3. You must speak words of success, abundance, and achievement into your life as if it has already manifested.

We have broken these three steps down into examples for you.

Step 1—Becoming Clear

I am celebrating my personal freedom! I no longer feel any burden or suffering in my life, in my business, with my health, or in any of my relationships. I have completely detached from my stories of unworthiness, and I believe in myself and show self-care and self-love in all of my actions and thoughts. I have a fulfilling relationship filled with love, reciprocation, and adoration, and my partner treats me like a princess. I am tended to and looked after; I feel heard and valued. I have more money than I even know how to spend! I constantly write cheques to worthy causes and enjoy the feeling of helping others through my success. I spend my time working on projects that inspire me. I collaborate with inspired and intelligent people from across the world, and I am building new and exciting friendships every day. My children are thriving, float easily into every stage of their lives, and are balanced and healthy human beings. I feel amazing and look even better. This lifestyle of no stress and no time pressure is serving me well! My life has never been this peaceful, and every day I am effortlessly continuing to grow into the best person I can be!

Step 2—Feeling the Manifestation into Reality

Close your eyes and listen to yourself saying your manifestation statement. Does it make your heart sing? Do you get excited and warm in your heart, and does a smile spread across your face? If the answer is yes, then you have just birthed your manifestation. You have given enthusiasm and life to your goal and dream; it is now on its way to being delivered to the universe. Just like clicking your send button on an email, you have notified the universe that you would like this in your life.

If the answer was no, please return to step one and get into deeper details about your goal and dream. Dip into all the nitty-gritty until you find the bits that light you up like a Christmas tree—the parts that make you able to see and feel how amazing this will be when it manifests into your life.

An important note to run alongside step two is that manifestation is deeply personal and intimate. Manifestation does not occur from a place of ego—that is, a place where the goal or dream needs to be validated by others. Manifestation is private, and as you feed and tend to your manifestation in your internal world, the excitement and energy builds. It is like an intimate secret that you are holding away from others, until it is so big, so exciting, and has materialised so that you can burst out and share it with others.

When you share with others your goals and dreams, you open yourself up for criticism, jealousy, and judgement; others may comment on your happiness. This need for external validation is fed by the ego, but true personal success is measured and validated by the self, not by others.

Have you had an incredible idea and shared it with someone, only to have it pulled apart? You walk away feeling deflated, have low self-confidence, and abandon that idea or dream because you perceive it as a bad one. This is why manifestation has to be private. It is a private secret between you and the universe, something that you talk about together and continue to connect with. It involves those happy and positive feelings that come as you imagine and feel the goal or dream materialise in your life. Stay centred in these happy feelings, and at the same time become innately aware and take personal responsibility for any negativity, self-doubt, or stories that emerge as you manifest. If these stories come up, do the techniques we shared in the first section of the book. Practice watching these stories and behavioural reactions instead of engaging in them. Apply a disassociation principle— that is, see your triggered emotions as outside of yourself; see them as a program that has been running but that you can make an empowered decision to discontinue. When you view these emotions as outside of yourself and consciously choose to no longer have them as part of your experience, you detach from this reaction. This technique is powerful and assists you in moving into the now and creating the future with a different experience. This disassociation technique disconnects you from the behaviours and emotional reactions of the past.

Do not tell anyone your ideas, goals, or dreams until you have committed 100 per cent and have seen the initiation of their materialisation. Once you can see this proof around you, then begin to speak words of light, enthusiasm, and gratitude for its materialisation. Before you speak, ask yourself why you need to speak. Do you need validation by others, or is your commitment questionable? Sometimes we tell others our story to receive their judgement and projection, if we are looking for an excuse to walk away from our goals and dreams. Ask yourself what your intention is in sharing your manifestations, and watch your ego!

Step 3—Speak Words of Abundance, Success, and Enthusiasm into Your Manifestations

We always like to speak words of gratitude over our manifestations. For example:

> I am so grateful and happy that my manifestation of my new black Audi is coming to be. I have visualised, felt the emotion, and am now sitting in readiness for it to materialise. Manifesting is easy! I deserve incredible things in my life, and every positive and evolving goal and dream that I manifest gives me even more confidence and validation that I am living in my true creativity. I love manifesting joy, happiness, abundance, and opportunity into my life.

Every day when we wake, we visualise and speak words of confidence into our dreams and goals, whether it be lying in bed with our eyes closed and feeling and visualising what it is like to be living our manifestation, or speaking words of life into our dreams and goals in the shower.

Nic chants in the shower, "I am love, I love myself, I am worthy, I am passionate, I am amazing. I enjoy personal and financial freedom. Money and opportunities flow into my life effortlessly as I commit to being the best version of myself. I am a patient mother. I am in creation of my life in all times. What I think about materialises. I am supported and fearless. Nothing ever goes wrong in my life." Nic is always listening to and reading affirmations, and therefore they come together in the form of one long, personal mantra every morning in the shower.

Ali likes to sing. She often has music and songs in her head that she sings, which empowers her. Ali also has on replay in her mind every morning, "I am stepping up, claiming the space, and being the best version of myself. I choose creation, not reaction. I am amazing."

As we have shared before, every two hours the alarm goes off on our phones, and we listen to recorded affirmations. You can also read out your personal manifestations at these times. Always begin with manifestation in the present tense, as if it has already materialised. Begin your statements with "I am …"

Do you like to shop? Here is a fun exercise for you to do each and every day. We are all worthy and deserving of all that we believe is possible in our hearts. We like to think of life as one big online store. Every moment of every day, we are "shopping" with our energy. Our energy and intent is our currency and how we "buy" things in our online store. Allow yourself to open your mind and come with us for a moment.

The Internet is limitless; you can type anything into Google, and it will come up with details, information, and images. So too is anything possible in your life. If you can see it in your mind, feel it in your heart, and imagine it in your life, then it can and will be yours.

Come and play shopping with us! As you go about your daily activities, drop off your children at school, drive to work, walk past people on the streets, pick up your dry cleaning, and shop for your spouse's birthday present, be aware of *everything*. Do your best to get out of your thoughts and the to-do list in your head. Become an observer. Become a hardcore intentional shopper.

Allow your energy and your intention to be your currency, and allow yourself to make purchases in your global and limitless online store. Imagine that everything you see before you is coming up as a possible purchase in your online store. Your Internet connection, your thoughts in your mind, is solid and running at high speed. This Internet connection never disconnects; it is there every moment of every day, if you wish to plug into it. With everything that you see and give your attention to, you send a message to the search engine in the online store, and a full display of information and images comes up for you. Make a decision whether this is important to you, whether it matches one of your desires in any area of your life. If so, place it in your shopping cart. Allow yourself to click the buy button, and put in your specification for the colour, model, and delivery date. When you play this shopping game in your life every day, it becomes effortless to manifest anything.

Let us give you an example from Nic.

> While driving my daughter to school, I drive past a black Audi Q7. As I notice this lovely luxury car, I consciously connect into my online store and click "buy now." As I walk into the arcade where my clinic is, I see a beautiful couple sharing a morning coffee and holding hands. I click the buy now button—that is, I set the intention for more intimate time with my husband on a weekday. Every time that I receive a sale in my online store, I say, "Thank you, universe," and click the buy button in my online store for more sales and the effortless flow of abundance into my life. I collect my daughter in the afternoon after school, and she tells me of a friend who just came back from

a camping weekend in the Grampians. I click "buy now" because I would love to manifest the same in my life.

This online shopping game works for every aspect of your life, not just manifesting material things. Every time that I read a blog or watch an interview on YouTube, I click the buy button because I want to manifest the opportunities of the people being interviewed by people I admire. This is how we manifested this book. We dreamed of being authors and having a book that could be a synopsis of all we love, believe in, and care about. Each time we met an author or read a book in our genre of finance and self-help, we clicked the buy button. Before long we had manifested an opportunity to attend a writers' workshop. Not long after that, we manifested the how with the correct publisher, and soon after that we manifested the time and beautiful space to write this book. Each part of this process was through the online shopping game.

Ali likes to play this shopping game with shoes, earrings, and dresses. However, she does a great job of materialising opportunities and meeting people through the online shopping game. When we attended Oprah in Melbourne, Ali had been playing this shopping game for months, manifesting our opportunity to meet her. Of course the universe always delivers what we ask for, so we were sitting having our breakfast and watching her do her morning workout with her trainer. She then waved at us on the way back to her room.

Everything that is around you is on offer to you—every T-shirt that you read, every garden you drive by, every mouthful of food that you swallow. Everything in life has infinite beauty, and they have no limitations other than what you place on them. As such, it's so important to remain open and connect with the magic that is around you at every moment. We speak to our children in this way too. We tell them that what they think about materialises, and therefore they should go to school knowing that they are going to have an amazing day. Nic's seven-year-old now says on the way to school, "I'm going to have an amazing day today, Mum." This is the power of intention and creation.

Give yourself permission to be playful, to walk around with this constant Internet connection in your consciousness, and to begin shopping. If you walk around consciously with this intention in your life, you will be amazed at what will effortlessly show up for you in your life.

> *I choose to focus on the new, creating effortless success and abundance for myself.*

What brings you peace? What would your life look and feel like if you believed that it could be peaceful? Success when you actively choose and create it to be is peaceful. Success does not need to come with struggle, does not need to be an upward battle, and does not need to contain conflict, chaos, or confrontation. Who decided or activated that program within you that climbing to the top was hard work?

What if it could be different? What if your business could grow exponentially and with ease? We have made a commitment to each other that we will only pursue opportunities and ideas that are effortless. We no longer want suffering or difficulty in any aspect of our lives. Everything can be loving, and everything can have a perfect grace and flow when you choose it to be so. This requires constant intention as well as stepping into the action of creation every day, creating ease and peace, and creating success and financial flow with no limitations. Stepping into this creation process at least 51 per cent of the time can be all that is needed to tip the balance and bring peace and ease into your life.

This creation needs to be done with commitment. You must step into creation with your business every day. That means setting intentions for every hour, every encounter, every meeting, and every relationship. For example, as you are driving to work and thinking about your day, be in creation. Think thoughts and speak words of ease and grace, such as, "My staff meeting today is going to be effortless. I am going to resolve any conflict with love, and I am not going to be taken by surprise by any confrontations from my staff." Similarly, when you think about your upcoming meeting with your accountant, create a positive outcome with your intention. Speak words of ease about your meeting, and note that there is always plenty of money to go around and the business is never lacking in anything. "I always have the right people, know-how, and timing in my business. Success and growth is always effortless for me."

Committing to this personal flow through setting intentions results in plenty of celebrations! When you apply this consistently and hold yourself accountable to this new way of doing business, you will have plenty for which to be happy and grateful.

We have learnt that successful business occurs first in the mind. When you create and set intentions in your mind, they materialise in the outside world and into the experience you have in your business.

When Nic was twenty-three, she borrowed ten thousand dollars from her dad to build a clinic. It was a big step for a young, passionate natural therapist who had just graduated from college. It was an even bigger leap of faith for her dad to invest money into a clueless but inspired entrepreneur with no business or marketing plan! Nic's dad shares the story of how he leant her the money with no expectation that it would ever be paid back—after all, isn't this what one did with daughters? Nic remembers a conversation while she was at college. Her dad did not really understand her course material or anything about natural medicine. The conversation was very left-brained, with him trying to remain open-minded and supportive of Nic's career choice. All the while, he had thoughts and feelings inside that said, "This doesn't make any sense." After all, he was an engineer, and what made sense to him was dollars, cents, and spreadsheets! He eventually learnt that natural medicine has lots of proven results; it is very scientific and has a long, proven history. Over the thirteen years that followed, he became Nic's greatest advocate. He has had countless ailments healed and resolved from her formulas, and now he seeks natural therapists for the maintenance and management of his health. He is in incredible shape for sixty-two years young and continues to make more empowering and right-brained choices about his wellness and lifestyle every year, including water fasting, meditation, practicing mindfulness, and committing to nutritional supplements and Puraforce Remedies. He even uses a pendulum and has crystals in front of his computer to protect him from electromagnetic frequencies!

Nic paid her dad back within a year, and the rest is history. But how? Through manifestation and mindfulness! After all, back then Nic had no skills in copywriting, advertising, or sales funnels! All she had was her genuine desire to be of service, and her naive enthusiasm. At the end of the final day of building and painting, she said all of her thank-yous, locked the door, and then burst into tears. Everything she had wanted and had been manifesting was done, but now she had to pull it off. Nic sat in the middle of the clinic floor surrounded by her certificates and the beautiful décor, and she made a pact with the universe. "Okay, universe, I did as you inspired me to do. I have followed my heart, but now I have to pay back my dad. Let's make a deal, I will work my hardest to serve and heal every single person that you lead into this clinic. I will research, study, and work on these people until they are well, as long as you support me with continued security and divine intelligence." Over the months that followed Nic would sit in her clinic. When she didn't have patients, she would study the cases she did have until she had a treatment strategy that worked. She worked and worked, and after two years she had a thriving practice. Paying back her dad was a distant memory, and she'd created a thriving business, a dinosaur that needed to be fed. She created this with conscious intention. When she didn't have patients, she would meditate, practice mindfulness, and learn about manifesting. When she received a large bill, she would manifest the money to pay it. Nic sat in divine service, serving a higher purpose and a higher need to be of service. This same process began again when she was given the divine inspiration to transform her clinical formulas into Puraforce Remedies, the online store and presence of her work.

Follow divine inspiration with the belief and knowing that you will always be supported. First you have to commit to taking action on the inspiration. That is the first step to the materialisation of your goals and dreams. Allowing yourself to grow into and through the process of manifestation.

Nic and Ali's collaboration as the Entrepreneurial Babes has had the same evolution. It was an initial concept based on an inspired idea. We then stepped up into action to create something that we had been dreaming of: a movement for women who supported each other's successes within the business world. Every day we continue to manifest according to those initial inspired ideas. The details and the projects continue to evolve because we are open to our limitless potential.

Celebrating each and every one of your manifesting successes is an important part of cementing the faith and worldly proof to yourself that you can manifest all of your heart's desires. If you are tentative to start, begin with something small such as manifesting yourself a car space at the supermarket, or winning a raffle. Once you have applied the steps of manifestation over and over again, you will grow into the process with increased ease and confidence. Like everything in the game of business, it is your commitment and consistency that will bring you the fastest and the most rewarding results!

As you step up, claim the space, and grow into the best version of yourself, you require support, encouragement, and directional learning. Nic and Ali have had personal and professional mentoring and coaching for many years. Each coach has enabled us to learn different skills and receive direction at major points of our businesses' growth. Without the guidance and knowledge of mentors, we would never have been able to scale and achieve what we have in such a small amount of time.

Choose your teachers well. We have experienced many coaches and coaching styles from many of the major psychological and mental educational models. It is very important to find the correct fit for your personality type and for the stage you are in at this present moment. In order to grow, you must feel nurtured and supported, and at the same time you should be held accountable and be stretched and challenged. At times this balance can be tricky to find. Coaching and teaching without a loving foundation does not stick; it is a confrontational and painful way of pushing rocks uphill. In order to release and move forward, you must feel safe. In our experience, it is impossible to do inner work and continue to stay motivated and move forward if you feel you are under attack or being criticised.

Often women who work with us have come out of this unloving foundation of business mentoring, and there can be emotional blocks that this kind of aggressive coaching can produce. Until you find it easy to love yourself and believe in yourself, being told that you are not good enough and that you are not performing can be an unpleasant and heartbreaking experience. For us, the bottom line is that you can't do better until you know better. In most cases, people who know better immediately begin to do better. There is not a problem with people or their commitment to their successes; instead, it is often a block or internal resistance, or a lack of information and know-how.

Our collaboration was created on the foundation of a loving friendship. For the first time in our lives, we had reached loving and constructive feedback, criticism, and advice in the business world. This was revolutionary to us at the time because we'd both come out of unloving and painful business coaching in the past. We discovered that there were multiple ways to climb to the top, but through our friendship, we grew faster and more effectively than before we had met. It wasn't that we were necessarily instilling new business ideas or know-how; instead, we were creating a platform of support and love that neither of us had received or were getting from any other relationship or coaching. This was where our global project was born: the idea that if we felt like this, then there must be thousands of other business people who felt the same. Surely there could be a different experience. This desire and divine purpose was planted in our hearts, and our lives changed forever.

We truly love each other, and it's a deep sisterly love that feels like it has many lifetimes of depth. The friendship that we share had to be celebrated! It had to spoken about, because the friendship has a rule book based on intellect and maturity. We were two women who were willing to put on our big-girl panties and be loving and supportive of each other. We were not intimidated or threatened by each other's successes, and we needed to find more women like us because we didn't want to go back to the days where we felt the jealousy and the put-downs from others while being unsupported.

We want to invite you to be part of our movement—a new collective consciousness of businesswomen loving and supporting other businesswomen. It's a true friendship based on respect and admiration, with no bitchiness or put-downs. It's a change in consciousness where women can collaborate and empower one another for the greatest benefits of the planet, empowering and leading the next generation of businesswomen into another way of business behaviour based on love.

What we know for sure is that women are the future. To transform the world, we empower and activate women because this has a ripple effect into every family across the world. By empowering, educating, and inspiring women, we have the ability to change and transform the ways and laws on which this current economic climate is set. By challenging the way things are done, by acting on divine inspiration, and by stepping into our own unique creativity, we have the opportunity to create a new dynamic business climate in which all of us can thrive. The talent, innovation, genius, and creativity of women have not even begun to be tapped. Imagine what will happen once this collective consciousness of freedom, liberation, and self-love travels into businesses, organisations, and corporate structures all over the world! We are excited about this day, and we predict we will see an engagement and pursuit of love, inner happiness, and contentment like never before. Women are a force to be reckoned with, and what if this force could be loving and transformational? What if, by creating this global collaboration and collective consciousness, we could inspire and empower generations of women to thrive and to have limitless potential?

Please join our global love consciousness by working and investing in yourself. Here is how you can contribute and be the change that you wish to see in your own life, your business, and your community.

1. Love yourself, commit to your self-worth, and know that you are a source of infinite potential, love, and genius.
2. Begin to share, express, and step up into your creativity. Commit to expressing your unique talents and creativity, and give yourself permission to share them with the world.
3. Be loving in everything you do. Let your actions and words be transformational. Be the force of love in your life! Be your own light, light up your business, and let your path of creativity change the planet.
4. Stop being a woman you cannot love. Stop all of your unloving behaviours such as put-downs, criticism, jealousy, gossip, and drama. Let go and pull apart all of the stories that keep you trapped in your limited beliefs about yourself and your business. Allow yourself to be infinite in your abilities, and celebrate other women's abilities and strengths along the way.
5. Celebrate who you are and what you are achieving. Move your consciousness to now, make your life self-serving, and contribute to this collective consciousness. Create a plan within your business where your successes can inspire, liberate, and create positive change for others. Build an orphanage, buy land and give it away to families in need, or save the whales. We all have a divine resonance with a particular cause. Step up, claim the space, take action, and be a part of your divine calling. Are you passionate about people, children, the sick, the hungry, pollution, animals, or injustice? Use your blessings to bless others. Build a business and empire that has a legacy outside of wealth generation.

6. Be the change you wish to see. Do not wait for someone else to take the action or to be the leader. If you are in business, you are a leader. Collaborate and join forces with other leaders, and live your life by design. Build your wealth, build your lifestyle, and be your own inspiration. You are your own million-dollar formula!

Entrepreneurship is living a few years of your life like most people won't, so that you can spend the rest of your life like most people can't.

—Unknown

CHAPTER SYNOPSIS AND CALL TO ACTION

- Step up, claim the space, and be the best version of yourself. Step into all you know you can be.

- Begin to manifest the life you are dreaming about with our three-step process.

- Stop engaging in negative commentary about other people. Celebrate others' successes.

Question to Ask Yourself:

Are you in creation, manifesting your dreams 51 per cent of the time?

Do not go past this section until you apply and conquer the information in this section.

I CHOOSE FOR
Myself

Today I step into the *knowingness* that everything is available to me. I choose only great things for myself, I choose *infinite possibilities* and I consciously open myself on every level to receive. I do not need to struggle or to push harder to achieve what I *desire*. I do not need to manufacture or work harder to obtain solutions. Everything is available to me and as such the *answers* always appear and all my *needs* are always met.

I always have *enough*, I always am enough and I always do enough. There is no need to question myself or to place doubt on any aspect of my *life*.

Nothing ever goes wrong in my life as I am always *supported*. I *trust* the process of life and *release* the drama, suffering and resistance I often create for *myself*.

I follow my *intuition*, I feel *confident* in my decisions and I *celebrate* the progress I have made *today*.

I receive *miracles* in my life everyday, as I *expand* my consciousness I see the *incredible* opportunities around me.

ENTREPRENEURIAL
BABES

PART THREE

Consistency

CHAPTER 7

Accountability Is Different To Consistency

What is accountability? It is a term that is often loosely thrown around in every aspect of your career, but have you ever stopped to think about it? Accountability is the process of following through; it is a personal decision about what you will commit your exertion to. In every moment, we have the choice to be lazy or to be active; this can be mental or physical activity. Accountability is following through and taking action on something that you have created in your life. Each time that you open your mind and engage in the world you have created for yourself, you are creating accountability because you are making decisions about what you are doing, where you are going, and with whom. All of the action and activity ultimately leads to exertion. Exertion is the energy it takes to do things.

We have worked with thousands of women who have low exertion; this means they are tired, feel depleted, lack motivation, and are generally uninspired. We are all given the same amount of time every day; it is our exertion and our output that differs. What you create for yourself and the level of connectedness you have to your inner creativity can greatly affect your exertion. Most of us have experienced this; we have high exertion when it comes to having a day at the beach with our friends, however our level of exertion is low when it comes to cleaning the house and maintaining the gardens.

Exertion is physical and mental, and as such we must fuel our exertion correctly. Low motivation, poor drive, apathy, and procrastination are symptoms of low mental exertion. Feeling tired all the time, having heaviness in your body, and having poor health are examples of symptoms of low physical exertion. When we are in this low physical exertion, it is very hard to get into action and be accountable and consistent in our lives.

Many people whom we work with have blockages and require coaching in this area. They do not have solid foundations set with a commitment to their health and wellness through hydration, nutrition, and exercise. Many people who seek our help are frazzled and overwhelmed in their business, and as such they have poor sleep.

These are the building blocks to creating high exertion for yourself. When you are in high exertion, it can be productive and consistent because your body and your mind can keep up with what you are making yourself accountable for. In simplicity, the level of exertion you create for yourself—that is, your energy—directly influences your output. This sounds super simple, doesn't it? However, how many of us actually commit to doing this consistently? Not many!

We go through the highs and lows of looking after ourselves, and our hormones and business realities, such as travel and busy periods, greatly affect these highs and lows. But what if you could create for yourself high exertion all the time, which would mean you could be more accountable, could take more on, have more yes in your life, create more opportunities, have more streams of income, and do it consistently?

You can! You simply have to choose it to be so. Understanding the exertion output ratio and how it affects your productivity is the first step. We have spent a lot of energy in the first third of the book empowering you with tools to increase your physical and mental exertion, and now you need to apply them. Take some action and decide to be the best version of yourself.

Unfortunately, this is part of the personal growth that we can't do for you. We can't be like Gumby and melt and transform ourselves through the pages of this book to make changes with you. All we can do is empower you with the information, tools, and techniques. We encourage you to start making better and more accountable decisions for your life and business. When you do this consistently, you get the results. Your life and business can be effortless and easy—if you choose it to be so.

We would love to be able to hold your hand through this and be the constant voice of reason and accountability. We can't be in your life, but we did write this book. This book is the kick in the ass, smack in the face, and truthful, no-fluff wake-up call that you may need!

This is what Nic and Ali do to each other every single day. We kick each other up the ass on a foundation of love, knowing that we both are truly committed to stepping up, claiming the space, and being the best versions of ourselves. Are you ready to make that choice for yourself?

When you make this choice in your life, you hold yourself accountable. You make yourself the biggest and best version of yourself, but you take no bull along the way. There is no room for down days or laziness anymore, because your heart wants more. You want the personal and financial freedom that we have been speaking about, and all of a sudden those lazy behaviours don't fit anymore.

You become a new person. Ali and I joke about our friendship: we spend so much time together that we have merged into this one person. We are so deeply in each other's heads, we are accountable, and we have unpacked and let go of so much emotional baggage that even our language has become the same! We are morphing into this loving, accountable, consistent, money-making machine, and can we tell you it rocks! Making the decision to have personal excellence and be accountable to our exertion was the day our lives changes. We became serious, and it was no longer an option to waste time. Ali stopped becoming so distracted; she stopped allowing herself to drift off, and she is a serious producer now. You should see the content and the outcomes of just one day! Nic has always been on super charge, but now she is even more committed. Her self-care, self-love, and personal health are transforming because she knows now that she doesn't have a choice!

Performing at the top level requires discipline! Do you want it enough? We do! We want the highest possible level of personal and financial freedom. We want the opportunity to travel more and worry less. We step up every day, claiming this space of personal excellence and committing to ourselves as a million dollar formula.

If it's meant to be, it's up to me!

So what are you waiting for? Oprah is one of Ali and Nic's greatest inspirations and says, "If you are waiting around for someone to come and rescue you or to help you, you are wrong. It is your job, your responsibility. You are responsible for your life and for your happiness." We could not agree more, which is why we get fired up. We want you to be the best version of yourself. Step up and get your life and business on track. The buck stops with you! It's time for you to commit to accountability.

Make a decision now: are you in, or are you out? Then you need to get accountable and into consistency. Ask yourself now whether your exertion or energy is high or low, and then make it change if needed. Be accountable to making a different choice to improve this area of your life.

We are not big believers in doing things in small chunks or slowly. The motto for our friendship is, "Go big or go home!" When you get yourself right—all the different areas of your life, including your relationships, your business, your children, and your extended family and community involvement—it falls into place like a magic row of dominoes. If you get yourself right by upping your exertion, improving your health and well-being, improving your mindset, stepping up to your divine creativity, and expressing your truth, then the magic will start to flow. Why? Because you have stepped into creation. But you have to do this consistently!

The best accountability for exertion is the level of suffering in your life. If you are surrounded by peace, happiness, and fulfilment most of the time, then you know you are nailing the creation process, your exertion is high, and you are accountable. If this is not the case, you have some work to do—some inner work! It's not about tidying up your business, getting more organised, or managing your money better. These all may need doing, but the first work is with you!

You are your own million dollar formula! As you master yourself, your life and your business are also mastered. Stop looking outside of yourself for answers. Commit to all the information and tools in the first section of this book. This is where you start!

You must do this work every single day. It is essential for your exertion and your output to be consistent. On the days that we do not commit to being accountable for our business behaviour, and on the days we do not practice mindfulness, gratitude, expression, and divine creativity, we crash too! We don't like crashing, and we know you don't either. Consistency and being accountable for all of your growth is what stops the patterns of highs and lows, of stops and starts. It's what begins the process of flow.

When you are in flow, your life is effortless. This effortlessness doesn't come without the work. What work are you willing to commit to in order to achieve the life you truly desire, the peace you know you deserve, and the personal and financial freedom you are longing for?

When you do the work, you get the results.

CHAPTER SYNOPSIS AND CALL TO ACTION

- When you do the work, you get the results.

- Be accountable for your growth. The change in your life and business starts by changing yourself.

- Consistency creates flow, which leads to effortlessness.

Questions to Ask Yourself:

What is your level of output and exertion?

CHAPTER 8

What Are You Willing to Commit To?

There is no such thing as an overnight success. The greatest artists, entrepreneurs, musicians, and athletes are not a result of one successful album or tennis match. These successful individuals have mastered consistency. They practice and practice, even when they don't want to, do not feel inspired, and are tired—and then they get up and do it all over again. Mastering anything requires sacrifice and commitment. Anything worth working for and dreaming about is worth getting uncomfortable for. Success doesn't come without you being uncomfortable. It doesn't come unless you are willing to do some work, and most of it is internal. What are you willing to sacrifice and commit to in order to achieve your dreams of personal and financial freedom?

We created the action hours. This is waking every day from 5:00-7:00 a.m. and working on yourself. Master your personal and internal dialogue, commit to a practice of gratitude, make a space to unpack, and release yourself from your stories. It's a place where a consistent rhythm and space in your life can be dedicated to you. You are your businesses success, and when you master yourself, your business will thrive! Are you willing to commit to 'the action hours' with us? Are you willing to sacrifice a bit of sleep to really stretch yourself to reach your infinite potential?

When we first created the action hours, we were encouraged by the enthusiasm around us. As we committed to the practice of meeting every morning at 4:00 a.m. in the middle of winter, to walk around our gorgeous Blue Lake in Mount Gambier, the people around us were inspired. They thought it was a crazy fad and would not remain a rhythm in our lives, but it has! We know that we are better together, and as such we walk and talk for an hour before we work together in the action hours. We then go home and get our children ready for school, drop them off to start their day, and head to work. We end our day at 3:00 p.m., collect our children, and do the nightly routine before opening our laptops again from 7:30-9:00 p.m. This is what we have committed to—our flow. This is our commitment to our success.

After a while, we started to attract a little bit of resistance from those around us. Once people realised that we were doing this consistently, that we were serious about our personal success, and that we would achieve complete financial and personal freedom in the next three years, we think they felt a little intimidated.

Nic is willing to give up her TV time, and Ali is willing to sacrifice her time on social media. We do not sacrifice our family time. Our husbands and children do not miss out. We are efficient, consistent, and accountable to each other and to ourselves in order to be the best versions of ourselves. We have built a weekly rhythm that serves us. We have laid the foundations with our health and well-being plan of natural medicines, nutritional supplements, green smoothies, exercise, sleep, and hydration. We do not feel tired and lethargic—it's the opposite. We are on fire! We have never been in better physical and mental health in our lives, and we are kicking goals!

We have made a commitment to be consistent, to do the same thing every day as the road to personal and financial freedom. We have spent hours analysing the behaviours and lifestyles of the rich and most successful entrepreneurs on the planet. These people set themselves up for success. They are efficient and on task, look after themselves, and have a work-life balance.

When we started to receive negative comments about our action hours, we were not offended because it was what was right for us. The movement we have created and the solid proof around the productivity and effectiveness of our cognition is well written about and proven. We didn't need any validation or approval from others; we did not seek the commentary of others. We do this for ourselves.

When you reach a state of flow and effortlessness in your life, and when you reach an inner peace that comes from knowing that you always have enough time, intelligence, and creativity, then you always have enough money and resources because you are always enough, and a shift internally changes.

Running our global businesses is not hard, impossible, or strenuous. It doesn't make us fatigued and depressed. We jump out of bed every morning on fire because our personal and financial freedom is on track. We are living the dream. We continue to create opportunities for ourselves, and we are inspired every day by the women whom we mentor. We see how their businesses are transforming and how their personal lives are becoming happier, healthier, and more peaceful. Trust us—there is no struggle here!

The question is, do you want it enough? Nic is pathologically driven, and she has always had many projects and businesses on the go. She has woken every morning early, her brain in gear and ready to go. For Ali, this transition was not as easy. She has always been a morning person rather than a night owl, but she is a processor, which means she takes times to digest things. Our brains work differently, and we work our businesses to leverage off these strengths.

When are you most productive? Are you a night owl or a morning person? When do you have the most mental clarity, least distraction, and most commitment to yourself? Most people we have worked with say it is in the morning. There is something deeply cathartic and intimate about working in the quiet of the morning, before the noise and the rest of the world wakes. There is space in the morning to dream, plan, and consider the possibilities. There is also space and time to process and unpack emotional baggage. There is opportunity to feel what you need to feel and let it go. The daily commitment to personal development and business success will become addictive. The journey to entrepreneurship is about commitment and sacrifice; it's about making choices that most don't make, so that you will have choices that most don't have later.

To those of you who are reading this now and feeling really challenged, we want to challenge you even further. What if by committing to the action hours for the next three years, you could be financially free and never have to work again? What if really mastering your self-worth, detaching from your stories, disengaging from suffering like drama and gossip, putting on your big-girl panties, and getting serious about your life and business could transform your life? What if you became committed to personal excellence, which then revealed an effortless flow in your business and personal life? What if it could be this simple?

We are here to tell you it is! The more consistency you show to this personal practice of getting up in the action hours five days a week, the more you'll practice gratitude and work on your business instead of in it, and this will transform everything. The people who are following us and committing to this practice every day see and feel this transformation in their lives. Come with us and be part of our movement of empowering yourself and looking within.

We are willing to make this sacrifice and commitment every day because we will be financially and personally free to travel, work on passion projects, and expand our charity work. Financial and personal freedom requires personal excellence, and if your personal stories of lack, pain, and suffering are the dominants in your life, you cannot move forward. Similarly, if you are stressed, overwhelmed, and feeding your business dinosaur, you are an employee on your own payroll!

It's time for you to get serious about your business. Step up and claim the space of your personal worth. Shift your business from a hobby or a little side income to the infinite potential you have. Make a commitment to have a million dollar business in the next three years by stepping up, claiming the space, and being the best version of yourself. You are your own million-dollar formula.

Your business is an expression of yourself, so looking outside of your consistency will continue to engage you in the suffering and lack in your business. Instead, we need to elevate and spin around our thinking to look within. This personal commitment to work on our inner world is often more frightening than working on the outer daily tasks of working in the business, because it creates vulnerability, and suffering does not lie!

Take yourself out to lunch and get serious about what you want. What do you want to have around you and for your life? If you were to create your life by design in the next one to three years, what would that look like? Design it, and then come with us and get serious!

Nic had been working in her business for over ten years, but she had never gone inside. She was always struggling, and there was great success and abundance around her, but it came with enormous exertion and a lot of suffering. Everything was hard because she believed that she never had enough—and most important, that *she* was never enough. Nic was great at making families well, and this was where her training laid. She was great at coaching and mentoring women, but she was working in a business dinosaur, where she experienced income capping and emotional and physical fatigue from working long hours in her business.

After endless marketing and business seminars, entrepreneurial intensives, workshops, and travelling around the world to learn from the best, it finally clicked. Nic was the common denominator for all of the suffering in her life. Nic continued to live in the story of not being or having enough. The most prevalent story was that she didn't know enough, and so the pursuit of entrepreneurial and business knowledge became an obsession. As fast as she was earning her money from her business, she was spending it on expensive education. Her commitment to learn more and find that million dollar answer was obsessive. Nic looked outside of herself for the breakthroughs, for that marketing strategy, for that perfect partner in business. None of this was the answer. The answer was in her physical and emotional pain, which she wore like a heavy backpack for years! This personal and consistent resistance, she took with her all over the world. This feeling of being unworthy followed her, as did her limited financial success. Then one day, it finally clicked!

You are your own million dollar formula. As you commit to unpacking your internal resistance, letting go of your suffering, and knowing you are always enough all of the time, the balance begins to tip to the 51 per cent. We do this consistently every day. We commit to personal excellence and shape our workdays better to have flow. Nic now stops when she meet resistance, and she dug deep to let go of all the stories. There were some doozies in there, like ex-husbands, financial loss, and lots of pain.

You have these pains too, and they are costing you! When Nic made the decision that she was enough all of the time, the money started to flow, the difficulty and the challenges moved out of her business, and her wealth began to build. When she stopped looking outside of herself for answers, consistent abundance and opportunities appeared.

Ali did the same thing. She was doing well in her role as a professional network marketer, and she created a positive impact on those around her, but she still experienced her business with resistance, and it was tough. Ali faced lots of resistance and adversity, and she took it all on the chin. There was plenty of criticism and suffering, and there were plenty of days that she wanted to walk away from this opportunity, but she persisted. Ali put on her big-girl panties and got serious about her own success. Like a horse, she put on her blinders and stopped listening to the commentary around her. She went inside, connected to her self-worth, and lived as the light that she is. She lit up her life and her business, and the more she connected into her light, the more money and opportunity flowed. She worked hard to detach from her stories, and the most challenging were around her health and family. She looked inside for the answers and did the work.

Our stories of suffering are different, but the action we took and the consistency that we show every day to continue this transformation is the same. We now experience abundant lives, and it is truly effortless, however our behaviours and our commitments have already been made. They have been set in stone like the foundations of our health and wellness. Your success is inside you! Creating commitment to go inside requires you to be honest and to get serious. Are you willing to do what it takes to let go and get uncomfortable? We wish we had a magic wand for you to make it easier, but we don't. Like us, you have to do the work. You have to be willing to back yourself, get uncomfortable, and make some sacrifices. Do you think Roger Federer got to the top of his game without getting uncomfortable? Absolutely not!

Your goals and dreams are on the other side of your discomfort. The breakthroughs are on the other side of vulnerability, and it may get messy for a little while. As you begin to shift, the people around you can get uncomfortable too, and they can be intimidated or unsure about your new language and behaviours. This discomfort is short-lived. When you create consistency about the decisions and actions you take in your life, they have an energy of their own. Your body and mind adapt to the early alarm, and it gets easier. The action you take becomes your formula for success, and the more you commit to it, the more you get out of it.

Nic is passionate about having no regrets in her life. She commits everything she has every day so that she never has to experience pain or disappointment as a result of not committing enough. An example of this was Nic's husband wanting to pursue a dream of completing a charity event in India, called the Rickshaw Run. In 2015 he went to India and rode a rickshaw across India with three of his friends for two weeks. The toll that this trip took on Nic's emotions and business was mammoth. It sounds like no big deal, but with preparation for a high season in her business and two young children, the opportunity could not have come at a worse time for her. However, she doesn't believe in regrets, and she supported him to do this. It had a wonderful outcome for him. Nothing is placed in your life without there being a reason for it. Nic dug deep and encouraged him to go. This is an example of getting uncomfortable. No growth or incredible achievement comes without a little bit of discomfort. You have to ask yourself whether you want it enough. Nic didn't want any regrets for him or for their marriage, and together they found a way.

What are you putting off in your life and business? Can you afford to do it, or are you willing to live with the regrets? Ali facilitates the balance for her husband to have several weekends with his mates each year. This is an important part of his health and well-being, and it aids balance in their marriage. It's not ideal for Ali to have the additional pressure of children and work as a single parent, but with consistency and organisation, it is successful for all. Where there is a will, there is a way.

We may be challenging you to get up early and miss a few hours of sleep each morning, but we are also challenging you to have discipline about your bedtime and not stay up watching television. You may need to catch up and bank some *Z's* on the weekend with an afternoon nap for a few weeks, until your body gets used to the new routine. However, the productivity and prioritising will have great benefits for your business. The question is whether you want financial freedom enough. Are you motivated by your creativity and your divine purpose enough to make some changes?

There's a difference between believing and knowing. When you believe in yourself, you think that you have the abilities. When you know in yourself, all the answers come out effortlessly. Shifting from a place of believing to knowing requires consistency. Challenge self-limiting thoughts and let them go until fewer of them surface every day. Begin with the big one: "I'm am never enough." We have identified that this is the biggest one there is for people. Believing this to be true is what holds you in your suffering and financial lack. Know that you are always enough, you always have been enough, and you always will be enough. You are on task with a divine purpose, and you have everything you will need at every point in the road. Know that you are exactly where you are meant to be at every moment, that you are in the process, and that there is not a final day that you are racing towards where you will have it all together. Right now you are reading our book, and this is exactly the part of the process that you are up to right now. You are divinely where you are meant to be. You are a work in progress. Trust this to be true and know it intimately, because it starts the shift from believing to knowing.

You will know whether you are still in a believing state if you still require validation from others. *Believing* you are okay and worthy comes from the ego. *Knowing* comes from the depth of your heart. When you know you are always enough, you feel it in every part of your being. This will be a process of growth. It still is for us. We are all works in progress. This is part of our commitment: to grow to a level of personal excellence where we know that we are always enough. We commit to growing into a place where personal resistance doesn't exist and where there is no ego or comparison to others, and there is gratitude and abundance. This takes commitment and daily practice in the action hours."

We start each day with a blank piece of paper. At the top we write, "I am so happy and grateful now that ..." Underneath this heading, we write all that we are grateful and thankful for; we write the personal and professional breakthroughs we are manifesting into our lives. The universe is hugely abundant and can deliver in an instant. We must know that we are deserving of all of the abundance, happiness, and bliss to receive it.

We also recite the Ho'oponopono mantra in our conscious thoughts. This powerful Hawaiian prayer says, "I'm sorry. Please forgive me. Thank you. I love you." It was best written about by Dr. Joe Vitale in his books *Zero Limits* and *At Zero*. We encourage you to read these books. They are fabulous resources for learning about the law of attraction and the Ho'oponopono mantra. This powerful technique and these books are very important regarding holding us in creation at every moment as a wonderful and powerful practice of mindfulness.

CHAPTER SYNOPSIS AND CALL TO ACTION

- Work with this affirmation daily: "I am enough, I have always been enough, and I will always be enough. I am exactly where I am meant to be right now."

- Practice the Ho'oponopono mantra every day: "I am sorry. Please forgive me. Thank you. I love you."

- Step out of believing and into knowingness. Move from your head space and into your heart space.

Questions to Ask Yourself:

What are you willing to commit to?

CHAPTER 9

How to Really Have It All

You really are allowed to have it all. The first step is to give yourself permission to have it all. You are allowed to have a deeply committed relationship, to wake up every day in your creativity and be excited to work on your million dollar business, enjoy your children, travel the world, have meaningful and connected relationships with family and friends, and even attain the trim figure for which you have been yearning.

The question is not about how to get it, but rather whether you believe you are worth it. You decide that your life is going to be everything you have ever desired. You choose for your life to be peaceful and for success to be effortless. If you don't decide, you will not create it in your life. Every single materialisation in your life comes from a thought, from you setting the intention.

When you wake up each day, do you groan and feel miserable for the first hour? Do you wake in a panic, full of dread about the day ahead? Do you wake feeling depressed and unfulfilled? If so, then we have some work to do. Your days will be just as you create them to be.

There is a very big shift that happens when you step into creation, but you must do it consistently, at least 51 per cent of the time, to tip the scales into a new possibility. When you wake and feel these feelings, you must start working straight away. You must throw yourself in the shower and snap out of it. "No! I do not choose to be tired and lethargic today. My body is fit and strong and supports my lifestyle effortlessly." When you feel that dread about the day ahead, speak words of intent over your feelings. "No, universe! I do not intend to be overwhelmed and afraid today. My life is balanced, and I gracefully shift from one part of the day to the other, feeling peaceful. Success is easy for me, and making money is fun." Speak words into your day when you are driving the children to school and heading to work. Nic says, "Girls, we are going to have an amazing day today. You are going to have so much fun at school." When driving to work, she says, "Today is fun and effortless. Money and opportunity come to me effortlessly, and I connect from my heart in all I do. I truly make a difference. My staff are happy and healthy, love their jobs, and continue to feel fulfilled in assisting me to create positive change."

Ali starts her day by setting her intention about her health. "I am fit and healthy. I am the healthiest I have ever been. I am amazing, and I choose to break the cycle with my health." She also sets this intention with her boys as they leave for school every day. "I am amazing, I am happy, I am awesome. Don't let anyone steal your greatness."

You must actively create what you want. This million dollar lifestyle is not going to turn up in your letter box. Do you want this? Do you want all you have ever dreamed of? Then start getting consistent with what you are creating. This takes discipline, and that is why we wake in the action hours. We write in our gratitude journals, we work on vision boards, and we are serious about not being in this same place in twelve months' time. You can begin to create this too.

We have the opportunity to speak to thousands of people every year, and the biggest conversation we have is around creation. We focus on the light within everyone, and after we walk away from meetings with business people, we see nothing but infinite potential. We need to get out of our own way! You are your biggest obstacle to happiness, better health, and the life you desire. At some point in the road, there has been a story, and your brain is stuck there like a bad traffic jam; it hasn't chosen to get on another freeway to take a different route to the city. Also you have not wanted your dream enough, because if you had, you would be there already. If 51 per cent of the time your thoughts were on your dream being fully manifested and the bliss that comes from it, and you were working towards it, then according to the law of attraction, it would have materialised for you.

Are you ready to get committed and consistent in order be the best version of yourself? It takes daily consistency to want and create something better. Start right now. What are the sabotaging thoughts in your mind? What story is in replay about how you are not good enough, or how this all sounds too easy? Or is your mind talk something like, "These women are whack jobs. It's not that easy! It can't be true. This will never happen for me."?

What will you choose to do? Will you get out of your own way and start being consistent in order to create change? Speak words of success, peace, and happiness over your life. Do this all day today, all day tomorrow, and every single day that you wake up breathing! This is what Roger Federer did. He picked up a tennis racket every single day, year in and year out, and his consistency and belief in himself was how he created his own success. Yes, he created it! It is not just raw talent or luck. There is no such thing as luck—there is only creation. You make your own luck. Look at the life around you. Are you creating luck? If not, step up, claim the space, and start creating luck.

We lovingly hold each other accountable to this fact each day. We kick each other's asses—Nic mostly kicks Ali's, if the truth be known—because we demand excellence for ourselves every day. You never know when your time in this physical body is up. We all have a limited amount of time, with only twenty-four hours in a day. We are opportunists! We want every opportunity, every drop of happiness, and vibrant health. We want deeply committed and loving relationships, more money than we know how to spend, and an international travel schedule based on fulfilling work. We seek family holidays and a charity arm to our businesses that impacts thousands of people worldwide. You can have it all if you get up and start doing the work!

You can't be offended by someone kicking you up the ass; you can't make it personal. In business there is no room to take things personally. Business is the divine expression of yourself, and there is nothing more authentic than this. When you put on your big-girl panties, do the emotional work to unload the emotional baggage there is nothing to be offended by. When you do the work and are authentic then you don't become triggered in your business. You have maturity in your work life, and you understand that making money is not personal. It is all your potential! If you have emotional baggage, you cannot attract wealth. It honestly is that simple!

You don't get to the top by acting like a pork chop, being offended, being emotional, and carrying on about your staff. Put your on big-girl panties and do the work! Give up your TV time or your sleep-ins; get serious about your time management and productivity. Make every day joyful, fun, and effortless, because you created it to be so. Do this consistently.

Create your own accountability, and don't look outside yourself for validation. As Nic says to Ali, you don't need a goodie-goodie badge! You get satisfaction and fulfilment from the success. Stop looking outside for the pat on the back when you have woken up five mornings a week for the action hours. What are you, five years old? This is your ego at play. If you need congratulations about creating the success in your life, then we encourage you to look at your stories around worthiness. What we know for sure is the success that comes from doing this work, and doing it without telling others or having the ego at play, is the best goodie-goodie badge out there.

Confront the truth about your failures and start doing something about them. It is your personal responsibility to change your life, your family, your health, your business, and your happiness. It is *your* responsibility.

What are your passions? Right now, give yourself permission to pursue them, even if it's just during the action hours and working on them in your journal. In your mind, see and feel what it will be like when it is manifested. Create a vision board. Commit to this practice daily and be consistent in your efforts and your desires to create it for yourself.

When two runners run a race, it is the one who desires it the most who wins. It is not the skills, the training, the nutritional support, or the natural athleticism. These are factors as to why they are good runners, but the runner who wins is the one whose desire is the most consistent. It is the runner who feels herself winning, can feel that celebration, can feel the knowingness that she has won, knows she deserves it at the core of her being and has created it to be.

What can you feel? What can you feel already manifested in your life? It's time. We encourage you to step up, claim the space, and be the best version of yourself. You are your own million dollar formula!

CHAPTER SYNOPSIS AND CALL TO ACTION

- You can have it all when you are willing to get up and start doing the work.

- Wake up and start every day with intention.

- Business is not personal. Do not be offended by feedback— embrace it and use it as a tool to pursue personal excellence.

Questions to Ask Yourself:

Do you need to lovingly kick your own ass into gear?

Step up, claim the space, and be the best version of yourself. You are your own million dollar formula!

STATEMENT OF
Intention

I am celebrating my personal *freedom*. I no longer feel any burden or suffering in my life, in my business, with my health or any of my relationships. I have completely detached from my stories of unworthiness and I *believe in myself* and show myself self care and self love in all of my actions and thoughts.

I have a fulfilling relationship filled with *love*, reciprocation and *adoration* and my partner treats me a like a princess. I am tended to and looked after, I feel heard and valued. I have more money than I even know how to spend. I constantly make contributions to worthy causes and enjoy the feeling of *helping others* from my success.

I spend my time working on projects that *inspire* me. I *collaborate* with inspired and intelligent people from all over the world and I am building new and exciting friendships every day.

My children are *thriving* and they continue to flow easily into every stage of their life. They are balanced and *healthy* and have infinite potential. I feel amazing and I look even better. This lifestyle of no stress and no time pressure is serving me well. My life has never been this *peaceful* and every day I am continuing to grow into the best person I can be, *effortlessly*.

ENTREPRENEURIAL
BABES

JOIN OUR *Movement*

Please join our global success consciousness by working and investing in yourself. Here is how you can contribute and be the change that you wish to see, in your own life, your business and your community.

1. Love yourself, commit to your self worth and know that you are a source of infinite potential, love and genius.

2. Begin to share, express and step up into your creativity. Commit to expressing your unique talents and creativity and give yourself permission to share them with the world.

3. Be loving in everything you do. Let your actions and/or words be transformational. Be the force of love in your life! Be your own light, light up your business and let your path of creativity change the planet.

4. STOP IT! Stop being a woman you cannot love. Stop all of your unloving behaviours such as put downs, criticism, jealousy, gossip and drama. Let go and pull apart all of your stories that keep you trapped in your limited beliefs about yourself and your business. Allow yourself to be infinite in your abilities and celebrate other women's abilities and strengths along the way.

5. Celebrate what you are and what you are achieving. Engage in a collective consciousness where your needs are met and you are also serving others. What this means is to create an arm or plan within your business where your successes can inspire, liberate and create positive change for others. Build an orphanage, buy land and give it away to families in need or save the whales. We all have a divine resonance with a particular cause. Step up, claim the space and be the best version of yourself. Take action and be a part of your divine calling. Are you passionate about people, children, the sick, the hungry, about pollution, animals or passionate about injustice. Use your blessings to bless others. Build a business and empire that has legacy outside of just wealth generation.

6. Be the change you wish to see. Do not wait for someone else to take the action or to be the leader. If you are in business you are a leader. Collaborate and join forces with other leaders and begin to live your life by design. That is, build your wealth, build your lifestyle and be your own inspiration. You are your own million dollar formula!

ENTREPRENEURIAL
BABES

Printed in the United States
By Bookmasters